MW00987559

FAY JONES

THE AMERICAN INSTITUTE OF ARCHITECTS PRESS
WASHINGTON, D.C.

THE ARCHITECTURE OF E. FAY JONES, FAIA

FAY JONES

ROBERT ADAMS IVY, JR.

CONTENTS

First published in the United States of America in 1992 by
The American Institute of Architects Press
1735 New York Avenue, N.W.
Washington, D.C. 20006

Printed in the United States of America
Second Impression, 1992

Library of Congress Catalog Card Number 92-18065
Cataloging in Publication Data is available

ISBN 1-55835-075-6

Design and type composition by *Group* C
NEW HAVEN / SAN FRANCISCO
(BC, DK, GS, CT)

Text for this book was set in ITC New Baskerville using small caps and old style figures; titles and subtitles were set in Copperplate Gothic 33

Printed by Hoechstetter Printing Company, Inc.
Pittsburgh, Pennsylvania

Front cover: Pinecote Pavilion
Photograph © Timothy Hursley

Back cover: Fay Jones, 1990
Photograph © Michael Bruce,
Maguire/Reeder, Ltd.

Half-title page: Stoneflower
Photograph © Timothy Hursley

Contents page: Pinecote Pavilion (left)
Photograph © Timothy Hursley;
Pine Knoll (right)
Photograph © Ezra Stoller/ Esto

Back flap: Fay Jones and Robert Ivy
Photograph © Michael Bruce,
Maguire/Reeder, Ltd.

Endsheets: Monaghan Residence,
screen door with stained glass inserts
Drawing by Fay Jones

Page 31: Cooper Chapel
Photograph © Timothy Hursley

Page 96: Stoneflower
Photograph © Balthazar Korab

It must be almost forty years since I first saw a Fay Jones house, which was, I think, somewhere near St. Louis. I remember thinking it was beautiful—that it had rich and mysterious spaces, with a kind of compression and expansion that hardly anybody but Frank Lloyd Wright seemed to have mastered. There were fiendishly ingenious details, especially wooden lighting fixtures, that had been made by repeated cuts on a circular saw. Astonishingly, the whole thing was reputed at that distant time to have cost eight dollars a square foot.

During the posturing and howling that have marked the architectural scene in the decades since, it has been a source of ongoing reinforcement to me to know that Fay Jones was continuing to make mysterious and magical places, yet places that always remained basically economical and practical. Even as the houses became larger and more spatially complex, they never lost their simple and honest virtues.

Years later, I had a chance after a lecture at the University of Arkansas to stay for a few days with Fay and his wife Gus just as Thorncrown Chapel was coming out of the ground. It was rather casually included in the tour they took me on to Eureka Springs. When the chapel was finished, and dazzled every architecture jury in sight, then clearly the time was right for Fay's extraordinary talent, at once familiar and amazing, to become public—celebrated in books and magazines worldwide. Suddenly the secret was out and the wonderful works of Fay Jones were the center of public celebrations, culminating in his 1990 AIA Gold Medal.

I have no real excuse to congratulate myself that one of my continuing enthusiasms for all these decades has become a national historic treasure. But it does make me proud, even thrilled, to see that this powerful and special genius who embodies nearly all the qualities we admire in an architect has become a part of the public realm.

Charles W. Moore, FAIA
Austin, Texas, Spring 1992

Encountering Fay Jones's buildings in the fullness of their Ozark settings startled me. Prior to 1987, when the editor of the AIA Press asked me to consider writing a book about Jones's architecture, my perception of this fellow southerner's work had been formed by a slide-show and by brief magazine articles. Neither medium had prepared me for the richness I would meet.

A visit to Stonelodge, a private residence in Hot Springs, Arkansas, illustrates my experience. My wife, Holly, and I were accompanied by Fay and his wife, Gus. As we climbed the hill on a brilliant fall day, a three-dimensional fullness unfolded in the architecture around us. No photograph could capture the complete sense of orchestrated space present in that one residence. Words, however, could relate the built object with my experience, helping the reader conquer the camera's two-dimensional limitations. A book could do that.

Further trips reinforced my early conclusions about Jones. The self-confident man stood apart from his contemporaries with singular authority; the stature of his buildings exceeded their scale. After conversing with Jones beside his smoky hearth and with his partner, Maurice Jennings, in their Fayetteville office, after rambling through the Arkansas hills on springtime site visits, I discovered a powerful body of work, a profound architecture in a superficial age, that demanded to be shared with a larger audience.

As Stonelodge startled me, Jones's best buildings share the power to move others. These inanimate objects affect the emotions and elicit a spectrum of feelings in the viewer quite independent of either objective analysis or sentimentality. Perhaps the release these buildings offer, like true art, partially explains public admiration for Jones's work, removed as it is from most of the twentieth century's architectural agenda of utility, historicism, or cultural relevance.

Strong architectural ideas, learned from several of this century's most forceful practitioners, lie behind the work. In small, specific ways, Jones's craftsmanlike wood and masonry buildings examine humankind's relation to nature and (by extrapolation) with its place in the larger cosmic order.

The "principles" he espouses, which hark back to Frank Lloyd Wright and earlier architects, evoke a universal harmony present in the physical universe; when apprehended and arrayed in houses and chapels, that harmony resonates through the work. Jones's work is inclusive, incorporating and repeating congruent themes at small and large scale into a total statement of universal order.

The principles inform the architecture, Jones insists. Therefore, I have attempted to explain his ideas as they have been presented to me. With brevity, I have sought to place the architect in a historical context, as well as to describe some of the experiences that formed this complex man's life. Where relevant, I have sought to explicate the work like verse—to describe the materials and methods that make the buildings what they are. My primary goal has been to open the work up to nonarchitects, amateurs in the sense of those who love architecture for its own sake. By describing the physical settings, the quality of light, the spatial effects invisible in photographs, I have tried to bring life to inanimate objects.

Books like this are seldom read serially, as one would read history or a novel. Because I have ordered the chapters into self-sufficient pieces, I believe readers will be able to pick the book up, put it down, and pick it up again at a later time without diminished comprehension.

I have introduced the architect and his work through a series of short essays that lay the groundwork for better appreciating Jones's buildings and their settings. Examples of his work, which follow, have been organized into two parts. The first presents chapels and pavilions, the culmination of Jones's architectural achievement. A representative sampling of his more than 200 houses exhibits the breadth of his mastery, from highly dramatic spaces to subtle details. A discussion of his residential design techniques follows.

What no book can convey is the man's spirit. Fay Jones exudes warmth, graciousness, good humor, reason, and commitment to ideals. The greatest dividend in pursuing this project has been meeting and knowing Fay and Gus Jones—joyous individuals whose lives and principles have merged. I honor them in this book.

Robert Adams Ivy, Jr., AIA
Columbus, Mississippi

It has been my hope to have inspired among my pupils a personality or two to contribute to this work, some day, forms of their own devising, with an artistic integrity that will help to establish upon a firmer basis the efforts that have gone before them and enable them in more propitious times to carry on their practice with a personal gentleness, wisdom, and reverence denied to the pioneers who broke rough ground for them, with a wistful eye to better conditions for their future.

FRANK LLOYD WRIGHT
In the Cause of Architecture II

Fay Jones (center) welcomes Frank Lloyd Wright and William Wesley Peters to the University of Arkansas, 1958.

When Frank Lloyd Wright looked beyond 1914 "with a wistful eye," he spoke prophetically of a disciple then unborn. The pupil he hoped for, the architect of artistic integrity and personal gentleness he expected to contribute to the work, was to be another American of Welsh ancestry—Euine Fay Jones.

Jones's life and his work have been a series of considered choices: to become an architect, to study with Wright, to accept Wright's organic design principles, to remain in his native state of Arkansas, to practice and to teach simultaneously, and to limit his palette to a few building types. Jones has tenaciously explored Wright's principles, producing more than 200 variations on a central, nature-centered theme.

Seen in its fullness, there might be a temptation to dismiss Jones's work for its repetition and its lack of range: similar cabinetry details appear in multiple houses; stone columns are employed in building after building; several early interiors seem imitative of Taliesin. What sets this collective work apart? Why do individual buildings deserve publication and honor?

By choice, Jones's range has been limited to two major building types—houses and sacred structures. His repertoire includes no museums, no large office buildings, no civic buildings. Wild originality, what he calls "ringing the universal bell," has not been his goal. Like a Baroque musician, he has preferred to restrict his formal investigations within a given framework; his reinterpretation of Wright's principles has evolved, through time, into a distinctive body of work.

Even though a striking affinity, a visual similarity, connects Wright's and Jones's work, Jones's own ideas pulse through even his early houses. Jones's persona flavors his architecture—a passion for the history of architecture, an engineering background, a strong work ethic and concern for pragmatic detail, an active, independent intellect that has ranged across philosophy, and a self-effacing concern for clients.

In the last decades of the twentieth century Jones has, more than any other Wright disciple, fulfilled Wright's wish, contributing an architecture with "forms of his own devising." History and archetype have inspired his finest houses, history's lessons rather than historical forms or appearances providing a framework for expression. Jones's diminutive chapels and pavilions rank among this century's finest expressions of ecclesiastical and public art.

Jones's carefully crafted work for a few individuals, reiterating the slow pace of human touch, may seem anachronistic; yet in another sense, his work may seem prophetic. By pursuing a humane architecture at home with nature—nonintrusive, respectful of place, harmonizing with elemental forces—Jones reminds us that we are merely visitors in Eden and that we should tread lightly here. ▲

In the future, . . . whatever the source of our creativity, we have the potential to build buildings . . . that will not only accommodate our functional needs, but will stand as models for the best of our ideas. We have the power and responsibility to shape new forms in the landscape—physical and spatial forms that will nourish and express that all-important intangible of the human condition at its spiritual best. As architects, as transformers of the landscape, we *must.*

FAY JONES

JONES'S PLACE IN CONTEMPORARY ARCHITECTURE

> It has been an issue of choices . . .
> I felt I was somewhat outside the pale.
> I knew how to do hyperbolic paraboloids, brutalism, and so forth; they were choices. But I feel you can choose to sit a dance out. I hate the term, 'not up to date.' If you are outside of peer pressure, you pick up [problems] and think about them in a different way.
>
> FAY JONES

"Outside the pale," Jones's admission of noninvolvement in contemporary ideological dialogue, sums up his attitude toward most contemporary building and frames an understanding of this architect's work. An individualist whose work has followed a steady path, Jones has maintained a calm voice through years of raging debate, clashing philosophies, and changing styles. The voice is firm with self-knowledge: Jones's path has been his own.

Removed from the trend-setting centers on the east and west coasts, the architect has been figuratively shielded by the Ozark Mountains from the pressures of fashion. In any review of the architecture of the 1960s, 1970s, and 1980s, Jones's work stands resolutely alone, revealing no parallel, no peer, and no apparent successor. Yet the buildings do not stand outside of time. Jones's own house shows the influence of the International Style. His buildings from the 1960s continually exhibited Modernism's concerns for revealing the true nature of construction materials through detailing and for simple building surfaces (planar walls, ribbon windows, and smooth countertops). And there is ample evidence of a consuming regard for workable solutions so that even the most complex details are designed around the capabilities of the electric hand saw.

From the 1960s, Jones's predilection for energy-conscious design is apparent in simple design choices: working windows, broad roofs, ample shade from deciduous trees, and proper orientation for light, wind, and shelter. Clerestories and skylights bring natural light inside virtually every Jones building and reduce the need for depletable fuels, doing without fanfare what contemporary polemicists whined loudly about. As concern for the whole planet rose in the zeitgeist, Jones brought a conservationist's sensibility to entire building sites: he disrupted the landscape minimally; his reverence and passion for nature are almost palpable in his work.

Irreverent ideologues other than Jones broke Modernism's stony hegemony. When in the 1970s debate and intellectual ferment, inspired by Robert Venturi's *Complexity and Contradiction in Architecture* (1966), gave rise to Postmodernism, Jones stood aside. There is a broad gulf between Jones's fully integrated work and early Postmodernism's tendency to shallow theatricality, but the movement opened the way to a wider appreciation of Jones's work. Jones thanks Postmodernism for "broadening the architectural vocabulary."

Polyglot might describe the architectural profession's recent language. In *American Architecture of the 1980s*, Andrea Oppenheimer Dean cited the decade's "wide-ranging eclecticism."

Literal historicism was accepted, Modernism was revived, and Frank Gehry's California abstractions flowered. Corporate America, aided by architecture firms like Kohn Pedersen Fox Associates, built the continent's urban icons—high rises that exuded 1980s confidence and wealth.

Big buildings were built for an expansive time, but Jones's projects remained small and iconoclastic. In this regard he was no longer isolated, as diverse talents with a sensitivity to their surroundings, from California to the Outer Banks, gained greater appreciation: Joseph Esherick of Northern California, whose Monterey Aquarium so beautifully captures time and place, won the AIA's Gold Medal; Antoine Predock's desert imagery distilled Southwestern regional and mystical traditions; W. G. Clark infused South Carolina's Middleton Inn with a symbolic Modernism redolent of Low Country ruins in a new age.

Although Jones's influence on recent architecture may not be explicit, other architects chose Jones as one of this country's "ten most influential living architects." In a national survey conducted by the American Institute of Architects in 1991, participants ranked Jones among a list that included I. M. Pei, Robert Venturi, Charles Moore, Michael Graves, and five others.

Reed Residence

In the same survey, Thorncrown Chapel emerged as the best work of American architecture produced during the 1980s. It headed a list of nine other diverse, seminal projects such as the Vietnam Veterans Memorial by Maya Ying Lin, Atlanta's High Museum of Art by Richard Meier, and New York's World Financial Center by Cesar Pelli.

Unlike some architects who produce verbose theory and rationale, buildings—not words—bear witness to Jones's beliefs. His art is tectonic rather than apologetic or descriptive, yet his very designs stretch the architectural dialogue. Pinecote Pavilion lighted at night cannot be easily dismissed.

A regionalist in the highest sense, that of an individual attuned to and responsive to place, Jones has interlaced placemaking within the larger tradition of organic architecture. ◬

THE EVOLUTION OF

PRINCIPLES

S. C. Johnson and Son Co.
Racine, Wisconsin
1936–1946

Fay Jones's singularly American architecture parallels his life story. To categorize him as merely regionalist is to misunderstand the man and his work. Nevertheless, place comes first, for Jones has persistently grounded his life in Arkansas, his birthplace.

Although southern in latitude and culture, Arkansas lies near America's spiritual heartland. Strong-minded, independent men and women settled the unspoiled landscape of rolling hills and clear waters, begetting a high-achieving progeny that would form the core of Jones's clientele.

Time dictated that Jones seek the most out of the least means; his childhood during the Great Depression forged an appreciation of economy. Jones was born on January 31, 1921, in Pine Bluff to Euine Fay and Candy Louise (Alston) Jones. The family soon moved across the state to Little Rock and later to El Dorado, a prosperous community in west Arkansas, where the elder Jones opened a small restaurant. Young Jones learned the work ethic alongside his mother and father in the family business.

While El Dorado offered few chances for him to pursue drawing or painting, Jones found ample opportunity to build. Salvage lumber from crates provided the material for an elaborate tree house with walls, a roof, a working brick fireplace, and even roll-up doors and screens. Although the tree house was destroyed by a stray spark, this childhood architectural experiment seems to have inspired subsequent treetop residences.

Jones found a window to the world beyond El Dorado in frequent visits to a movie theater adjacent to his parents' restaurant. One color short subject, a "Popular Science" film, inspired his career in 1938. The subject was Frank Lloyd Wright's then new Johnson's Wax headquarters in Racine, Wisconsin. "The film showed Pyrex glass partitions, curving brick walls, light pouring in. It felt like being thrown two centuries ahead in time," Jones remembers. For Jones, Wright's work united art and building, "the two things I liked doing. Architecture took on new meaning."

In a small state with few architecture firms and no school of architecture, the closest route to a career in architecture seemed to be engineering. Unsuccessful at obtaining a congressional appointment to the Naval Academy at Annapolis, Jones enrolled in the University of Arkansas School of Engineering, where he studied civil engineering for two and a half years. (His buildings would later express and integrate structure into their fabric.)

With war imminent in 1941 Jones withdrew from the university and tried once again for the Navy, this time as a pilot. He completed Naval flight training and was posted to the Pacific theater and to San Francisco. Of his experience as a Navy flier, Jones says he was "fascinated with the three-dimensionality of flight." (In Cooper Chapel and other buildings, Jones would achieve a soaring lightness and a precision akin to flight.)

While still a Naval officer, Jones made a lifetime alliance. On January 6, 1943, he married Mary Elizabeth (Gus) Knox, a native of Hot Springs, Arkansas. Even after two daughters, Janis and Cami, joined the family, Gus continued to manage the books and paperwork for Fay Jones's office, which she has done throughout his career as an architect. In addition, her warmth and intellect have stoked the fires of innumerable friendships.

At war's end in 1945, Jones, aided by the G.I. Bill, was, he says, "the first to sign up" as a student in a new architecture program started by Oklahoma A&M graduate John Williams at the University of Arkansas. He was to graduate in the first class of five people in 1950.

The year before graduation, Jones took a trip to see his hero Frank Lloyd Wright. "I had read everything I could about him," Jones recalls. "I could tell you the names and dates of his houses." The American Institute of Architects had at last selected Wright to receive the Gold Medal, its highest honor, at the AIA's annual convention in Houston in 1949. Hoping for a glimpse of the master architect, Jones and several other students encountered Wright "putting on his hat and cape" as he was leaving an AIA cocktail party in Houston's new Shamrock Hotel. Wright, who must have recognized Jones's panic at seeing him, introduced himself, took Jones by the arm, and announced, "This young man and I are going out to see the building." Jones says he realized, "I was going to be his prop." For thirty minutes the wide-eyed, twenty-eight-year-old architecture student and the octogenarian genius strolled through the hotel lobby, which was filled with celebrities for the hotel's grand opening, commencing a relationship that would take Jones and his family to Taliesin, Wright's fellowship headquarters in Wisconsin.

Gus and Fay Jones, 1990

A sojourn in Texas lay immediately ahead, however. After graduating from the University of Arkansas, Jones returned to Houston, this time to Rice University, to accept a fellowship and a graduate teaching assistantship in architecture. In discussing the academic courses that were most influential on his later work, Jones mentions not only his architecture studies in design, structures, and architectural history, but also his instruction in philosophy at Rice.

Next, Jones taught architecture at the University of Oklahoma for two years, from 1951 to 1953. His mentor at the university in Norman was Bruce Goff, whom Jones recalls as someone "completely dedicated to architecture." Today Jones's voice becomes animated as he discusses the intellectual setting at Oklahoma during the early 1950s: "I had never been at a school where there was such tremendous talent . . . such dedication to the work. It was the most artistic, exciting work I have seen to this day. It was an exhilarating time." He recalls Goff's passion for music, that recordings of works by Villa-Lobos, Ravel, and Debussy reverberated through the building and provoked discussion of music's relationship to architecture.

On one occasion, Goff acted as midwife to Jones's career by including him in a fateful, small faculty dinner for visiting master Frank Lloyd Wright. When the subject of Taliesin West in the Arizona desert came up in conversation, Jones recalls, he admitted to Wright that "I didn't feel complete because I hadn't been there." Wright responded with a hospitable "never too late" and an invitation for Jones to join him for the forthcoming Easter of 1953, which corresponded with Oklahoma's spring break. Jones drove to Taliesin West near Phoenix, where Wright soon expanded his offer, extending an invitation to the entire Jones family to spend the summer at the Wisconsin Taliesin. Despite the fact that Mr. Wright had neglected to warn Mrs. Wright that two children were included in the invitation, the Joneses were welcomed to Spring Green in May 1953.

Given two rooms in Taliesin proper, quarters adjacent to Chinese architect Ling Po and his mother, Madame Po, Jones and his family were struck by the intellectual commune that Wright

Taliesin
Spring Green, Wisconsin
1911

had created. "Every moment was an opportunity for creative effort," Jones says, from hoeing and weeding in the garden to evening musicales to baking bread. Although jobs in the fellowship usually rotated, once Jones had been assigned to the drafting room, he remained there. For the duration of his stay at Taliesin, Jones worked on plans for the Price Tower to be built in Bartlesville, Oklahoma, and on drawings and specifications for a house for Llewellen Wright, youngest son of the architect.

Interior, Taliesin

Although other Taliesin apprentices have related difficulties with the master, Jones found Wright easy to work for: "Mr. Wright had well-defined ideas, and everything reinforced his ideas." What Wright sought, according to Jones, was "simplicity, not plainness," echoing Wright's "yearning for simplicity" in his writings. In designing a building's foundation, for example, Wright asked, "What is the simplest way to do the next thing?" Jones never heard the supposed *enfant terrible* "raise his voice or seem displeased." Instead, Jones was drawn to Wright's "charm and presence," to his "beautiful command of the English language," and to his warmth and humor.

Jones and his family would keep their ties to Wright and Taliesin throughout the remainder of Wright's life, returning for annual birthdays or Easter pilgrimages. Wright reciprocated by visiting the University of Arkansas at Jones's invitation in 1958. The Joneses last encountered Wright at Taliesin West during Easter 1959, shortly before his death.

Today Jones freely admits Wright's strong influence on his work and his ideas, while he firmly maintains his separateness: "Understand I've never tried to become a little Frank Lloyd Wright. I'm not sure that it is possible to be a little Frank Lloyd Wright." While other Wright devotees have tried to advance his vision, Jones, by pursuing an independent path, has emerged from Wright's shadow.

Place played a role in determining Jones's identity. Taliesin had been rewarding and two years in Oklahoma had been fruitful, but something was lacking. "I felt that I didn't want to live in Oklahoma. I missed the hills," he says. Wright advised, "Why not go back to Arkansas? It is not as spoiled as the rest of the country. You can build there." In 1953 Jones and family accepted a call from John Williams in Fayetteville to join the faculty at the University of Arkansas, where a recently completed Fine Arts Center housed the architecture program. Fayetteville remains his home.

Although the new professor had been educated in the contemporary idiom and the principles of the International Style,

Maurice Jennings, Fay Jones's partner

Jones had experienced enough by the mid-1950s to maintain what he calls a "pluralistic approach" to education. He eschewed dogma, tempering his teaching with the reality and humility of practice, the career pattern he followed for three decades. Most afternoons, Jones would teach design and the history of architecture; on free mornings and weekends he would draw and plan buildings. The university became a refuge and inspiration; he reciprocated with loyalty and was installed as the first dean of the newly inaugurated school of architecture in 1974.

The teaching position allowed Jones the freedom to work and travel for three months of the year. University days and nights provided a "nurturing, creative atmosphere . . . in touch with people," he recalls. He mentions an evening spent with playwright Arthur Miller, a visiting lecturer, in the empty design studio where the two contemplated a model of a theater done in Jones's design class and speculated on ideals of theater design.

The University of Arkansas yielded one additional, valuable resource—a ready-made clientele. His earliest clients, including the head of the philosophy department, the dean of the law school, and a music professor, possessed a similar trait: they were creative individuals with low budgets. Jones quickly became known as "the guy who does faculty houses." A steady succession of residences followed the construction of his own house in 1956, permitting Jones to boast that he has never been without a commission since completing his first building.

As his work expanded, Jones needed help beyond his own two hands. Frank Doughty, Carroll Colvin, David Henderson, and a succession of former students occupied the drafting tables in the early days of his practice. While the size of the Fayetteville office has varied, Jones has intentionally kept its numbers and its complexity small, preferring to answer his own phone and to serve his own clients. A former student, Maurice Jennings, joined the practice in 1973 with John Womack, and remained to become Jones's partner in 1986. As Jones's travel time has increased with a more far-flung clientele, Jennings has maintained a steady day-to-day hand on the practice, overseeing its details and ensuring its accuracy.

Editors of national magazines, including *House Beautiful*'s Elizabeth Gordon, saw merit in the work of this small office. Beginning in the late 1950s, she and other editors featured Jones's residential designs frequently. These articles generated public interest before widespread professional recognition.

Recognition did come, however. In 1961 Jones received an award from the American Institute of Architects in cooperation with *Life* and *House and Home* as part of a "Homes for Better Living" program. Succeeding years brought further awards. Thorncrown Chapel (1981), the Roy Reed residence (1987), and Pinecote Pavilion (1990) won AIA national Honor Awards. Jones has received honorary degrees from four institutions: Kansas State University, Missouri's Drury College, the University of Arkansas, and Hendrix College. In 1985 he received the first American Collegiate Schools of Architecture Distinguished Professor Award. Particularly meaningful was the Rome Prize Fellowship, awarded in 1980, which afforded Jones time to study in Europe. The Joneses have frequently returned to the American Academy for visits and lectures.

Fifty-two years after Jones saw the film about the Johnson's Wax Building, and forty-one years following the convention during which Wright received the AIA Gold Medal and used Jones as a prop, Jones was honored with the same accolade. President Bush presented the 1990 Gold Medal to Jones at the White House, and Prince Charles of England attended the awards gala. The prince, resurrecting John Ruskin's terminology, praised Jones's poetry. Jones, who avoids grand statements, was typically direct and modest in his acceptance of the medal. His work spoke for him. Displayed on the walls of the great hall of the National Building Museum were photographs of Jones's simple, though not plain, houses, chapels, and pavilions.

Taken on the occasion of Frank Lloyd Wright's birthday, Spring Green, Wisconsin, mid–1950's. Left to right: E. Fay Jones, Aaron Greene, Katherine Lewis, William Wesley Peters, Virginia Loveness, Edward Durell Stone, Ben Raeburn, Maria Stone, John Dekoven Hill.

For Nature ever faithful is
To such as trust her faithfulness.

RALPH WALDO EMERSON
Woodnotes I

From a contemporary perspective, Fay Jones's architecture and concern for organic principles seem highly personal, even idiosyncratic. Yet his mature work represents a late twentieth century flowering of an evolving tradition that extends back 200 years. Romantic philosophers, led by Jean-Jacques Rousseau, and their literary popularizers unleashed forces still reverberating when they proclaimed the supremacy of nature. Equating nature and truth, they made nature the criterion by which all phenomena are united.

In *Emile* and other writings, Rousseau explored the education and development of individual personality, of originality, and of genius. In what author Donald Drew Egbert calls an interest in "the uniqueness of the individual human organism," human reason, which had held sway since the Renaissance, succumbed to feelings, to emotion, and to intuition. The writings of Goethe and William Blake parallel a change in the ruling architectural order from a classical system based on mathematical models to a pluralistic melange.

Emerson and the transcendentalists, who had a strong influence on Wright, furthered the discussion in this country. Speaking of the "useful arts" such as architecture, Emerson referred to nature as "the omnipotent agent," representative of "the universal mind." All art, according to Emerson, must complement nature, in which beauty, necessity, and usefulness are conjoined. Architecture, like poetry, takes on a deterministic quality: nothing is arbitrary; everything is necessary.

Emerson explicitly describes organic (that is, natural) architecture: "We feel, in seeing a noble building . . . as we do in hearing a perfect song, that it is spiritually organic; that is, had a necessity, in Nature, for being; was one of the possible forms in the Divine mind, and is now only discovered and executed by the artist, not arbitrarily composed by him." To achieve these ends, he admits the necessity of laws and principles derived from nature in art, principles that Wright would explore and expound upon and Jones would accept.

The overriding, inclusive principle Jones learned from his mentor, a self-professed Romantic, was organic architecture, a broadly defined concept. Though Wright himself danced around a definition, he frequently described its attributes in conversations, in lectures, and in his books. Wright sought through organic architecture a coordinated, interrelated design: "the thing is organic which has entity, in which *the part is to the whole as the whole is to the part*, which is the condition of life in anything," physically and spiritually, "true to the nature of man."

Fidelity to nature, and therefore to truth, is organic architecture's touchstone. Wright maintained that organic architecture should grow and evolve naturally. Buildings, according to Wright, should emerge from the ground with the sense of belonging and the dignity of trees. While the Indo-European root of the word *truth* signifies *tree*, "organic does not mean having a building look like a bush," as Jones has stated. "It is the central generator." To both Wright and Jones, the goal was and is natural harmony; integration, not imitation.

I'm always pleased to have the opportunity to acknowledge the influence of Frank Lloyd Wright.

FAY JONES

The spirit of organic design suffused and informed major and minor decisions throughout Wright's designs, as it has Jones's. Wrightian hallmarks that Jones adopted include simple, yet sophisticated floor plans which minimize wall separations, concentrate on spatial flow, and achieve a sense of connectedness to the exterior; openings interlocked into each wall's structural and formal rhythms; large overhanging roofs that shelter inhabitants while relating to the out-of-doors; an absence of such "dead spaces" as attics and dormers.

Organic design encourages decoration and integration of decorative elements into the whole building's structure and pattern, obtaining unity through complexity. Custom-designed pieces, both built-in and freestanding, furnish the rooms; unvarnished woods, rough stone, and other natural materials are employed. Muted earth tones dominate interior coloration, with an occasional vivid accent ("Go to the woods and fields for color schemes," said Wright). Indirect lighting knits walls and floors together; accent lighting from wall-mounted lanterns and chandeliers complements the overall design scheme. Low walls and floors contain integral mechanical systems.

The interior walls and colors of a Jones residence conjure up Wright at Taliesin. However, departures from Wright appear even

Above the Clouds at Sunrise
Frederic E. Church
1849

The beauty . . . of a building lies in the obvious adaptation of every part . . . directly to the stability of the whole, to which the position, dimensions, and form of every part must have so necessary a relation that, . . . if any one part were taken away, the whole would fall to pieces.

ARTHUR SCHOPENHAUER

in Jones's earliest buildings, differences as varied as articulated structural systems and the influences of other historical periods and other architects.

Jones has said that he feels fortunate to have inherited principles, "so there is a kind of continuum to join into instead of feeling that you can revolutionize and do things that ring the universal bell." The Romantic legacy adopted by Wright has been the framework on which Jones weaves his own response.

Specifically, Jones's buildings respect nature. He emphasizes that buildings should begin with "individual place." In the best work, "the building and site achieve a kind of oneness, a harmonious ideal relationship." He uses the words "fitting" and "belonging" when he describes how buildings and building sites should harmonize.

In a time when the people of the world have polluted the earth's waters and slashed its forests, Jones's respect for nature has been quietly consistent in his work. His buildings respond to the natural forces surrounding them to evoke, as Prince Charles noted, "the amplitude of nature—without damaging nature." His concern for environmental wholeness throughout three decades of international neglect may appear prescient unless seen as part of the Romantic legacy.

Just as the Romantic philosophers saw the artist's role as revelation of the natural truth, Jones has consistently selected natural building materials and sought to reveal their innate attributes. He has minimized the types of materials he builds with, experimenting and honing the pieces to simple, structurally necessary elements. Thorncrown Chapel's dazzling complexity is immediately reducible to individual pieces of humble wood; Cooper Chapel's, to thin steel angles in tension. Although combined into complex spatial constructions, each member declares its identity and carries its own weight.

The result of Jones's reductionism is the interrelationship of each part to the whole. Like Wright, who abhorred decorative detail applied in the classical manner, Jones fuses necessity and ornament in his architecture. Thorncrown Chapel embodies the nineteenth-century Danish philosopher Schopenhauer's definition of architectural beauty.

While an abstract, sculptural quality may accompany the architect's search for simplicity, all Jones's work is grounded in specific materials, places, purposes, and people. Like the Romantic artists who preceded him, Jones focuses on the individual in his work. He has designed no high-rise towers, multifamily housing, or new towns; not by chance, this university professor (universities encourage "individuality," according to the architect) has produced more than 200 private residences—customized shelter for individual clients. Wright expressed the intellectual basis for Jones's choice of building types when he wrote, "Our ideal is Democracy, the highest possible expression of the *individual as a unit.*"

Other elements of the Romantic tradition, nationalism and an interest in national cultural characteristics, arose concurrently with European Romantic philosophy. Jones's work for each client is identifiably American. In this century most movements have tended to universality, from Bauhaus architecture, which produced an International Style undifferentiated in India or in Indiana, to Postmodernism, which has drawn from classical antecedents, to Deconstructivism, which seems to reflect some global angst. Jones has avoided "isms," achieving through his very specific architecture an ever-widening appeal.

Jones's work, though grounded in an inherited philosophy, has changed through time. Evolving, it eschews imitation, seeking to transform the nature it inhabits. Human made, in harmony with nature, distinctly American, conceived by a strong individualist for individual clients, Jones's organic architecture carries forward a philosophical, artistic tradition. At its best, it accepts the Romantic legacy and moves beyond it, transforming the world one place and one building at a time.

I am not trying to imitate in any way. Architecture should announce the presence of art. It is human made.

FAY JONES

I sought some enduring qualities, something of the timeless qualities . . . .
I certainly never sought the novel or the bizarre . . . . I've never been interested in shock as a means . . . . Fads or trends are almost always misleading . . . .
I am trying to do work in a process that is based on time-honored principles.

FAY JONES

Kinkakuji (Golden Pavilion)
Kyoto, Japan
reconstructed 1954

Architectural precedent has guided Jones as a student, as a professor, and as a practicing architect. When Jones studied architecture during the late 1940s and early 1950s, schools of architecture, unlike their Beaux-Arts–influenced predecessors, de-emphasized architectural history. Contemporary architecture schools stressed instead the progressive dogmas and dicta of the International Style. Jones, who says he was "captivated by the history of architecture" in school, pored through and beyond the pages of Sir Banister Fletcher's books. When he began to practice architecture, his peers were razing the past for a brave new world; meanwhile, "I was quietly doing my own thing," he says.

Jones saw history not as an enemy but as a resource. The architect's responsibility, according to Jones, is not imitation, but reinterpretation; history can serve as a "generator" of ideas, not merely a source for copyists. In his concern for meaning, Jones realized that bridges to the future needed to connect to the past: "Any new building has the opportunity, perhaps the responsibility, to belong to the architectural continuum through the ongoing knowledge of themes and characteristics of architects who created the past."

Although Jones studied the full sweep of architectural history, he chose several periods, including the Gothic, as personal creative resources. He has not been alone. Wright and other proponents of organic design had admired the way Gothic architecture combined structure and ornament, its ornamentation intrinsic and evolutionary rather than arbitrary and imposed.

Like his predecessors, Jones's work shares kinship with Japanese architecture. The similarities, as others have noted, are striking: a reverence for nature with an emphasis on harmonious siting and landscaping; the employment of both still and moving water; a continuity between indoor and outdoor space; flowing spaces divided by simple screens; platforms that provide level changes within a single space; overhanging roof structures articulated by ridge poles; and natural woods emphasized by light-colored walls.

Rarely does Jones mimic a historic principle. He typically refracts the animating principle in a new light, accepting the axial symmetry of the Gothic cathedral, for example, but narrowing its dimensions. In some dramatic cases, Jones has turned the original principle inside out, in what he calls the "operative opposite."

Asked to plan a small city park structure for North Little Rock, Arkansas, the operative opposite principle guided Jones's design. For this small circular pavilion derived from a Classical model —the Temple of Hercules Victor (c. 120 B.C.) at Rome's Forum Boarium, he reinterpreted the classic column. Whereas marble columns sustain the roof's load in the original tempietto, in Jones's reinterpretation steel bars formed into columnlike rings have replaced solid columns. The earlier column's marble capital has been replaced with a pin; here, the steel column's core is hollow.

Sketch for gazebo column
North Little Rock, Arkansas
1970

Inspiration comes not only from academia, but from an awareness of the forms found down gravel roads. For the Roy Reed residence, the familiar barn offered a comprehensive model. Both the barn's climatic aptness and its form find new expression in Jones's hands.

As a traveler through architecture's past, Jones has appropriated ideas, but he has assiduously avoided pastiche. He works, instead, in a tradition, constantly renewing and enriching his individualistic architecture with scholarship, weighing cultural antecedents and the ideas of other architects as inspiration for new work.

Inspiration, whether direct or indirect, has come from a select cadre of earlier architects and critics. Louis Sullivan, Wright's *lieber Meister*, articulated many of the principles Jones espouses today. A philosophical kinship binds the two, although there is no obvious formal similarity. Sullivan rejected classical ideals derived from Greek prototypes that separated man from the universe, seeking instead a "peace with nature . . . the repose of absolute unity, the serenity of a complete identification." Jones has attempted to impart emotional and spiritual qualities Sullivan espoused.

John Ruskin, the mid-nineteenth-century English critic who through such influential books as *The Seven Lamps of Architecture* (1849) called for "honesty" in the materials and production of art, influenced several generations of architects, including Wright. Ruskin's admiration for Gothic architecture, expounded in *The Stones of Venice* (1854), would influence Jones's work over a century later. William Morris and the practitioners of the Arts and Crafts movement, whose American devotees included Gustav Stickley, in turn were influenced by Ruskin, as Jones would be by the craftsmen.

At the turn of this century, Stickley's magazine *The Craftsman* discussed "the integration of interiors," a concept in which all facets of interior design—from details to large-scale effects—were united by a single aesthetic. Sturdy, carefully wrought furnishings, lamps, incidental objects, and wood joinery were intended to complement the total interior. Design reached beyond the four walls of each building into nature; walks, low walls, drives, trellises, and pergolas extended the designer's hand.

The Gamble House
Greene and Greene
Pasadena, California
1908

Jones particularly admired the work of California's Greene brothers, Charles S. and Henry M., which was centered around Pasadena. The exteriors of Jones's early houses resemble those of the Greenes: wooden facades and broad roofs that partially shelter articulated stick construction. Like the Greenes' Japanese influenced houses, custom craftsmanship characterizes the interior designs of Jones's houses, including doors and windows, lighting fixtures, built-in furnishings and cabinetry, and dominant stone chimneys.

Unlike the Greenes but similar to Wright, hand labor for curving, molding and shaping, polishing, and pegging is minimized. Jones's interiors share a Wrightian spatial flow, whereas the Greenes' interiors, while characterized by more openness than their contemporaries, exhibit clear room divisions.

Another Californian, Bernard Maybeck, inspired Jones. Jones says his "interest was piqued" during World War II while stationed as a Navy airman in Northern California. Although Maybeck's stylistic range was broad, his work in wood and stone (at the Bingham house, Montecito, California, 1916, and the University of California's Hearst Hall, 1899, with its laminated wood arches) would later be paralleled by Jones's own work in Arkansas.

No American student of architecture during the late 1940s and no teacher of design principles during the 1950s was immune to the ideas promulgated by Walter Gropius and the Bauhaus. In language remarkably similar to the craftsmen and to Wright, Bauhaus ideologues spoke of "organic" building. Produced by "the collaboration of art, science, and technology," as Bauhaus theorist Laszlo Moholy-Nagy proposed, their understanding of the term "organic" architecture emphasized the social utility and function of the organic process.

The Kaufmann Desert House
Richard Neutra
Palm Springs, California
1947

Jones admits a particular admiration for Richard Neutra, the Bauhaus-trained architect who moved to Los Angeles in the 1920s. Neutra, who briefly worked for Wright during that decade, "reached out to embrace and intermingle with nature," as his biographer Thomas S. Hines explains. He placed particular emphasis on the continuity of space, a continuity that extended into the landscape. Jones, who met Neutra as a student and again as a teacher, today commends Neutra's mastery of interior/exterior relationships.

Jones also mentions his admiration for Harwell Hamilton Harris, a student of Neutra's. Harris's hillside residences such as the Ralph Johnson house in Los Angeles (1949), share many of Jones's hallmarks: board-and-batten siding, extended roof framing, glazed vertical end walls, and porches that are extensions of interior spaces.

Unlike the indirect influence of the Greenes, Maybeck, Neutra, and Harris, Bruce Goff's influence was personally impressed on Jones during his years as a fledgling professor under Goff at the University of Oklahoma. Goff looked to nature first for inspiration, drawing further energy from the related arts. He used painting, sculpture, primitive art, and music to impart compositional principles of rhythm, scale, depth, simplicity, and balance.

The Bavinger House
Bruce Goff
Norman, Oklahoma
1950–1955

Goff's seminal Bavinger house near Norman, Oklahoma (1950–55), was under construction when Jones taught at Oklahoma. Set beside a ravine, with the bottom level adjacent to the ravine wall, the house is locked into its site. Goff accepted the hillside into his composition, as Jones would do in the house he designed for his own family. Like Goff, Jones would integrate water features into the lower levels of his residences; like Goff, he would design a house based on the circle and a chapel based on the cone.

But Goff's primary lesson for Jones was intuitive, not explicit. Goff's is a naturalistic architecture filtered through a strong individual consciousness. Jones characterizes Goff's interests as "the strange, the unusual, the exotic," a reading of organic architecture that produced building forms that "began to look like organisms," while Jones's architecture became more geometric. Although their career paths diverged, Jones maintained interest in Goff's work, inviting him to the University of Arkansas every four or five years.

Before Jones met Goff, he had met Fayetteville native Edward Durrell Stone. Stone's influence on Jones would not be through design (although Jones admired Stone's programmatic skills), but professional and personal. "I felt a close tie to him," Jones says. If Jones's milieu was the microcosm, Stone's was the great world: from his New York office he collaborated with Phillip Goodwin on the design of that city's Museum of Modern Art (1936), the United States embassy in New Delhi (1954), and major corporate headquarters buildings. Stone broadened Fay and Gus Jones's world when he invited them to visit New York, to see his work, and to discuss his practice. He demonstrated, through a fully exercised life, what an architect from Arkansas could accomplish in the international arena.

SACRED SPACES

52. **MILDRED B. COOPER MEMORIAL CHAPEL**

92. **PINE EAGLE**

Give me the splendid silent sun . . .
Give me an arbor . . .
Give me nights perfectly quiet as on high plateaus . . .
and I looking up at the stars . . .
Give me solitude, give me Nature,
give me again O Nature your primal sanities!

WALT WHITMAN
Give Me the Splendid Silent Sun

EUREKA SPRINGS, ARKANSAS 1980

Thorncrown Chapel is elemental—a man-made temple married to the woodland. It rises with the authority of nature in the Arkansas forest from a stone foundation to wood columns and layered branches to folded roof. In plan no more than a single room, in form no more than a gabled shed, the small building draws visitors with the magnetic, irresistible force of truth. What Whitman calls "primal sanity," simultaneously rational and intuitive, integrates building with site, ornament with structure, and structure with form. This harmoniously unified masterpiece is arguably among the twentieth century's great works of art.

Jones recognized the chapel's potential as architecture, a distillation with the power to "move people in a special way," as poetry distills language. Although the building's dialect is obliged to Wright, Maybeck, and the Greene brothers (with an intangible debt to Japanese tradition), Thorncrown's authoritative strength comes from Jones's own voice speaking through the discipline of wood construction. Its language is American, tied to place and time, and, like Walt Whitman's verse, emerges from and evokes the American landscape and experience.

Like Le Corbusier's chapel at Ronchamp (1951–55), Thorncrown is a pilgrimage chapel, a place set apart in the landscape for meditation. Unlike Ronchamp, whose billowing white exterior suggests it might soar into the neighboring Jura Mountains and whose interior seems a solid, holy cavern, Thorncrown's peaked roof seems a part of the forest, its glass walls dematerialized by light and shadow.

The pilgrim, perhaps drawn to Thorncrown by a sense of discovery, is struck by the silence of its setting. On approach, leaves obscure the distance. Around a bend in the path, the chapel appears, caught by the sunlight like the largest tree. It seems both man-made and natural.

Light and shadow dapple the glass end wall; outside and inside, beginning and end, are blurred. An angular Gothic doorway opens on an interior forest of ascending wood. Overhead, crossed wood bracing fools the eye, extending a patterned perspective through the entire chapel.

Founder Jim Reed could not have foreseen the finished building's richness when he commissioned "a little chapel . . . to provide wayfarers a place for relaxation." His budget was limited; he loved his site, eight acres on a heavily wooded northeast Ozark slope, where rock outcroppings traced the contours. The building he dreamed of to cradle his ministry lies in a forest near heavily traveled

Highway 62, approximately two miles from the summer tourist colony at Eureka Springs, Arkansas.

Opposite: Light and shadow dematerialize the chapel's interior.

Jones transformed restrictions to opportunities. In order to save the trees, "early on . . . [we decided that] no structural member, for example, could be larger than what two men could carry through the woods," he says. Southern pine 2x4s, 2x6s, and 2x12s were employed; larger structural elements such as trusses were assembled on the floor slab and raised into place. Unified simplicity is achieved through interlocked, individual pieces.

Jones cites the "proportioning" and the "ascendancy" of Sainte Chappelle (1243–48), Paris's light-filled Gothic chapel, as inspiration for Thorncrown. Its single luminous space (24 feet by 60 feet and 48 feet tall), while smaller than that of Sainte Chappelle (32 feet by 99 feet), achieves a similar, grand effect.

Jones replaced exterior Gothic buttressing with interior, interlocking wooden arms to keep the exterior walls upright. The result is a reversal of the Gothic, Jones's oft-cited "operative opposite." Interior diagonal cross-bracing, which one critic called "a great lattice storm," carries the eye upward and animates the room. Hollow steel joints link the opposed cross-braces like bracelets. Repeated down the nave, these lozenge-shaped "oculi" produce a diamond fretwork of light; collectively they create the illusion of infinity.

A kaleidoscope of leaves and sky, seen through tall, clear walls and overhead skylights, suggest Sainte Chappelle's stained lancet windows. Jones, who says he "saw the potential for light play on the structure," enlarged the skylight on the roof's ridge to increase "the sense of drama."

Jones reduced materials to the absolute minimum: stone (flagstone floors and fieldstone perimeter walls), wood (structure), clear glass (walls), blue cloth, oak pews, and sculptural metal in incidental pieces (alms basin, door handles, lighting grates). Small details reinforce larger ones with the economy of a sapling. For instance, a cross motif appears in the metal bar stock supporting the pews, in lanterns lining the walls, in a metal column supporting the movable lectern, and in the chapel's cross—a slender metal stake positioned outside the transparent altar wall, symbolically connecting man to the universe.

Cross-bracing, showing diamond-shaped, hollow metal joints.

The small building has brought Jones international recognition. The 1981 AIA Honor Award jury noted, "One experiences pleasure and a sense of discovery upon arriving. Using minimal means, this chapel is a spiritual space." *Newsweek* reported, "In the

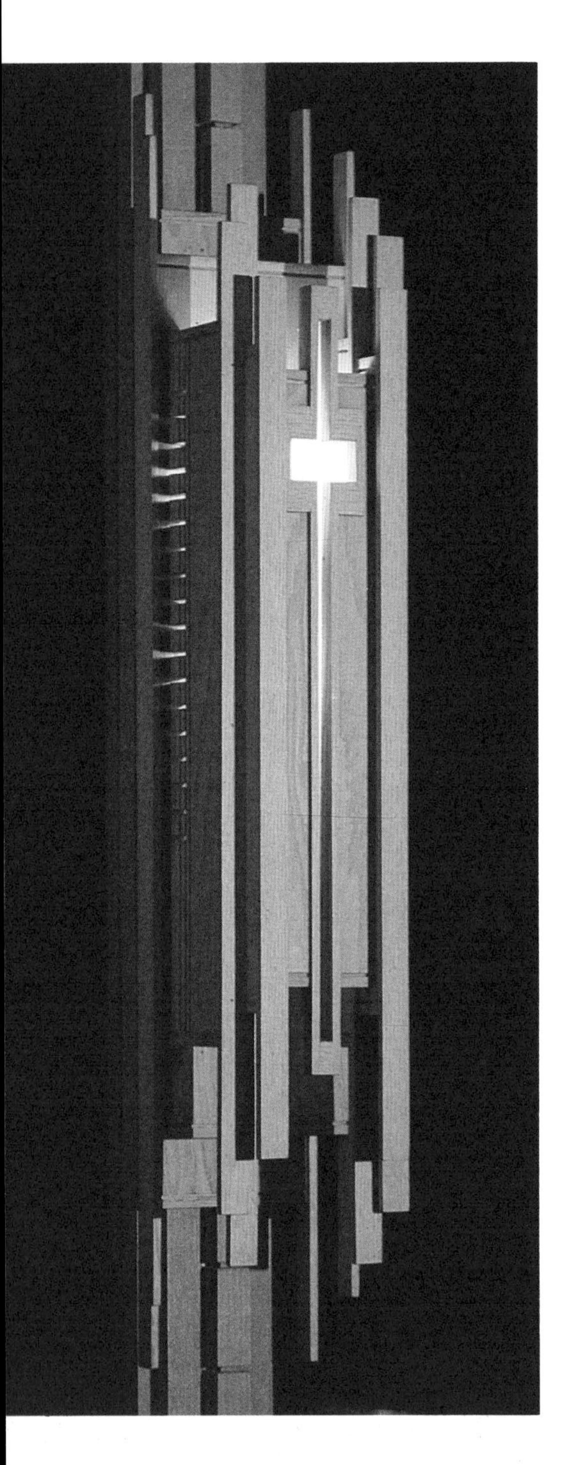

terms made famous more than 20 years ago by philosopher Mircea Eliade, Jones has reared a 'sacred' structure . . . a space that is not just physical, but metaphysical."

During certain times of the year, the small building draws more than 2,000 people per day up the slope outside Eureka Springs; Sunday services find 300 people present. They are attracted both by the building and by the harmonious truth the building points to; nature is manifest through Jones's architecture.

"I saw an opportunity here to create architecture," Jones says. "The distinction I'm making is that all building isn't architecture, just as all writing isn't literature or poetry, even though the spelling, grammar, and syntax might be correct. There is something in architecture that touches people in a special way, and I hoped to do that with this chapel."

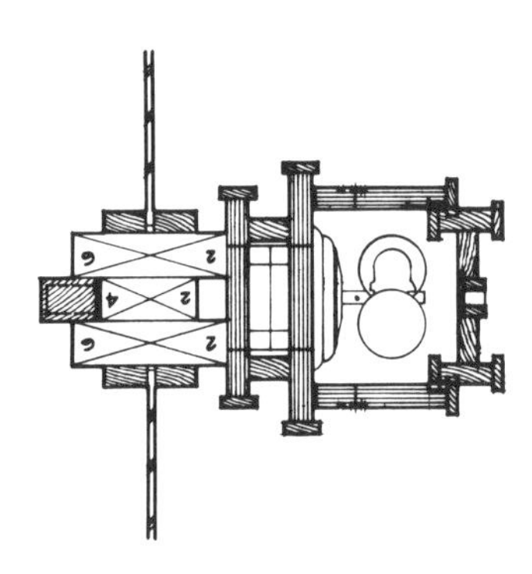

Twelve identical lanterns are attached to the columns lining each side of the nave. The detail at right describes a typical column construction, with an oak lamp shown within a glazed wall.

Opposite: Illuminated interior elevation.

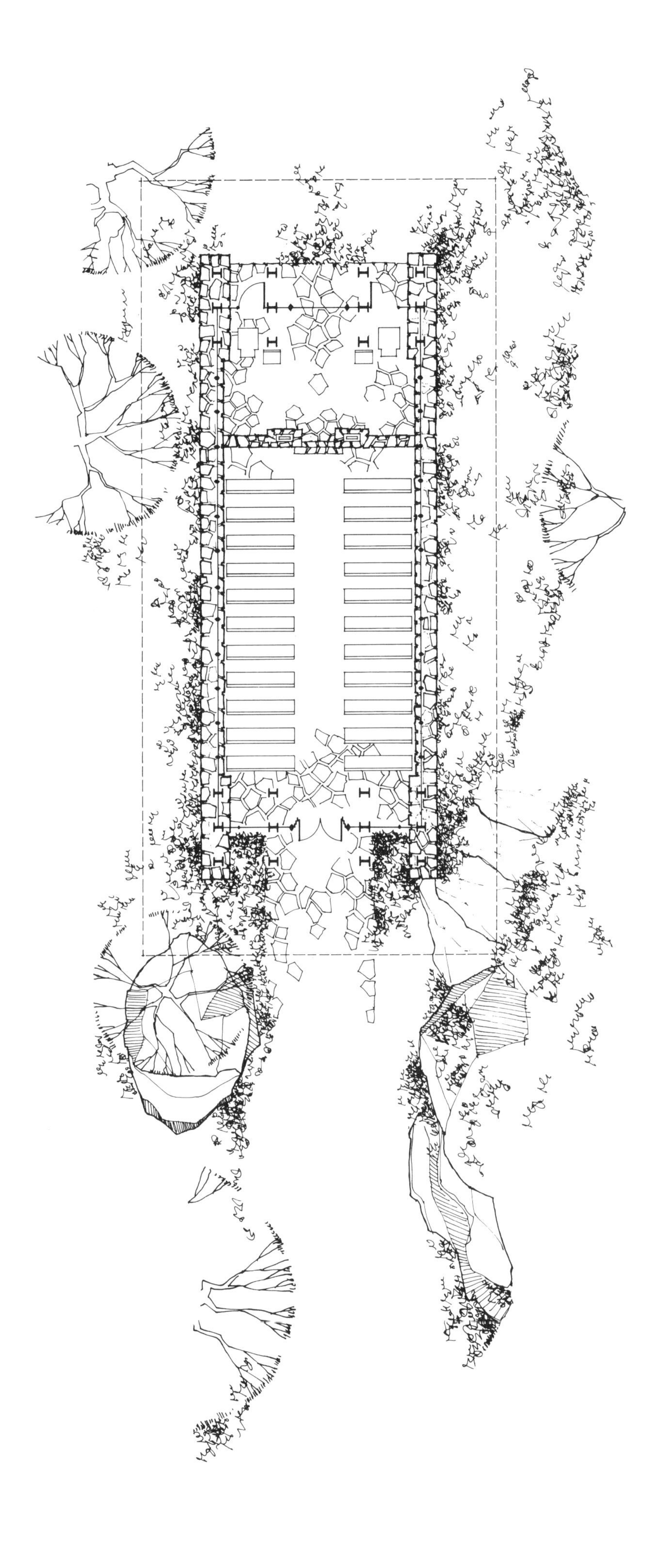

Plan. The site slopes from southeast (right) to northwest.

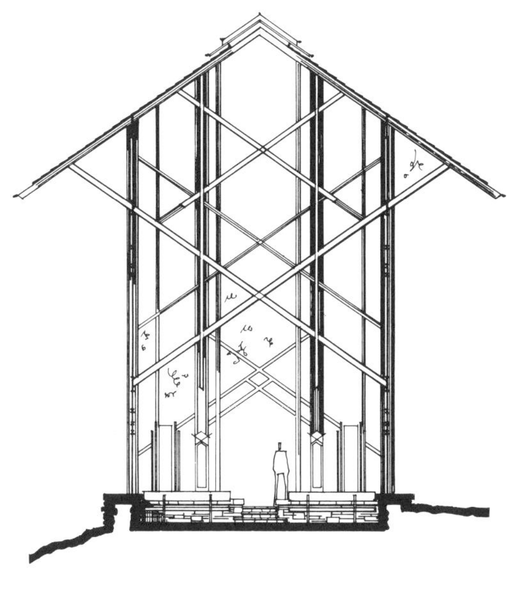

Section, facing northeast, showing interior framing.

Left: Diamond-shaped glass floats within the door frame.

The chapel's interior appointments include Wrightian ecclesiastical chairs and simple oak pews. Twin cabinets at the altar hold an acoustical system.

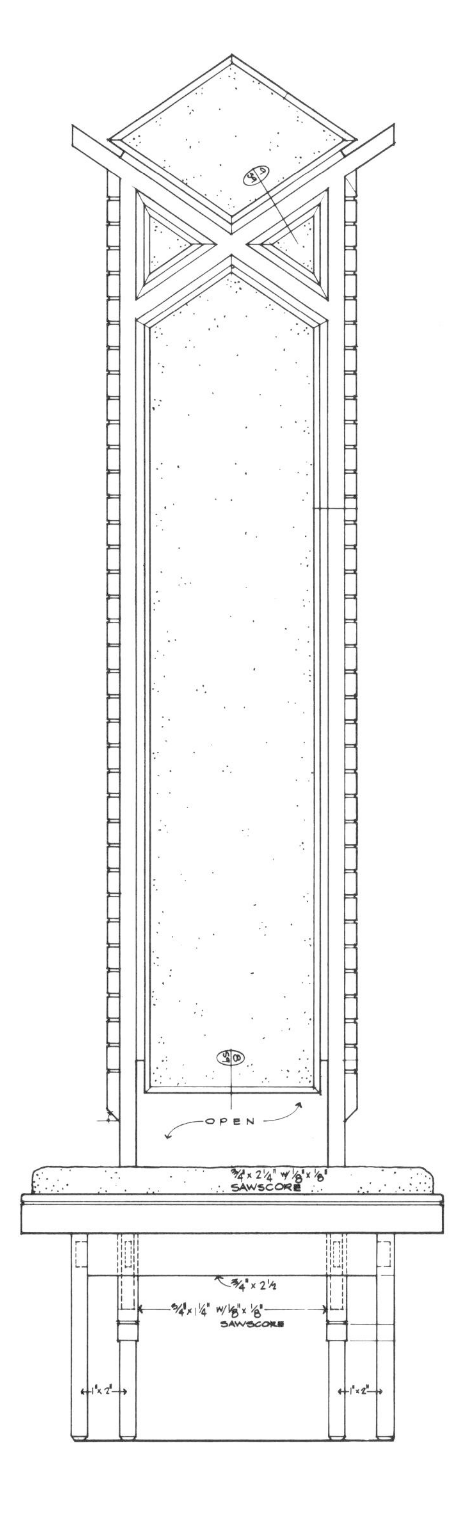

Exterior and interior cross-bracing knit the high vertical structure together. Vignetting results from repetition.

The silhouette of Thorncrown Chapel emphasizes its roof and framing.

Exterior at front door, looking through
window framing toward skylight.

Northern corner, where building and site cohabit a sloping hillside. Changing light and shadows continuously alter the viewer's perception of this pilgrimage chapel.

THORNCROWN WORSHIP CENTER

Thorncrown Chapel draws pilgrims from throughout the world to Eureka Springs, Arkansas, to wonder and to commune. When requests for wedding and worship services threatened to overwhelm the small building, the chapel's governing board called for relief. The client asked for a new sanctuary more like a traditional church.

The architect considered the problem, surveyed the potential building sites on the steeply sloping Ozark hillside, and placed a chapel in the air. The small structure, a needle-spired "church in the wildwood," stands on its sloping hillside site at treetop level —a very different solution from that of its woodland counterpart. The most striking differences between the two lie in their walls: transparent glazing opens up Thorncrown Chapel; wood siding surrounds the worship center.

Like the chapel, the worship center contains a single room. Like the altar of its relative, the center's altar is nature; a large mullioned tripartite window overlooks a chasm to the blue hills. Forty-eight feet wide, twice the width of Thorncrown, the building has solid walls that surround and protect the occupants, focusing all eyes on the services at the foot of the sloped-floor, 300-seat auditorium and beyond to the trees.

The walls are gypsum board with oak trim, their simplicity enhanced by the rhythm of customized wood lanterns similar to those found in the chapel. The chief ornamental element is a structural composition of scissored roof trusses. Surmounted by a linear skylight folded along the roof's ridge, the trusses' cross-bracing and pegged vertical members recall the depth and intricacy of stalactites.

The worship center does not depend on the chapel for identity, but juts boldly above the tree line. More pragmatic and less intuitive than the tree-shrouded chapel yet full of light and grace, the worship center frees Thorncrown Chapel for quiet reflection. ▲

EUREKA SPRINGS
ARKANSAS
1989

The worship center is enclosed in board-and-batten siding. Openings at each end focus attention on the altar and natural views of the Ozark Mountains.

A needlelike spire marks the chapel entry tower. The longitudinal section explains the chapel's sloping hillside site. Entry to the auditorium is at the upper level.

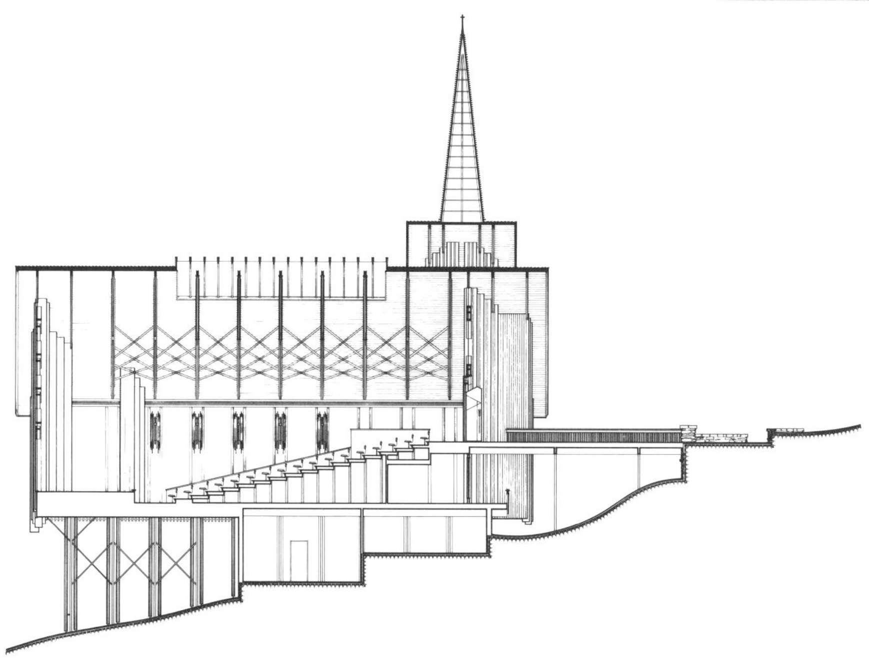

Above: Roof trusses enliven the space. Vertical chords explode into multiple members.

Left: View of the sloping sanctuary, looking toward the altar.

A pedestrian bridge connects the chapel with a walkway to the parking area. The forty-eight foot width of the sanctuary is twice that of Thorncrown Chapel.

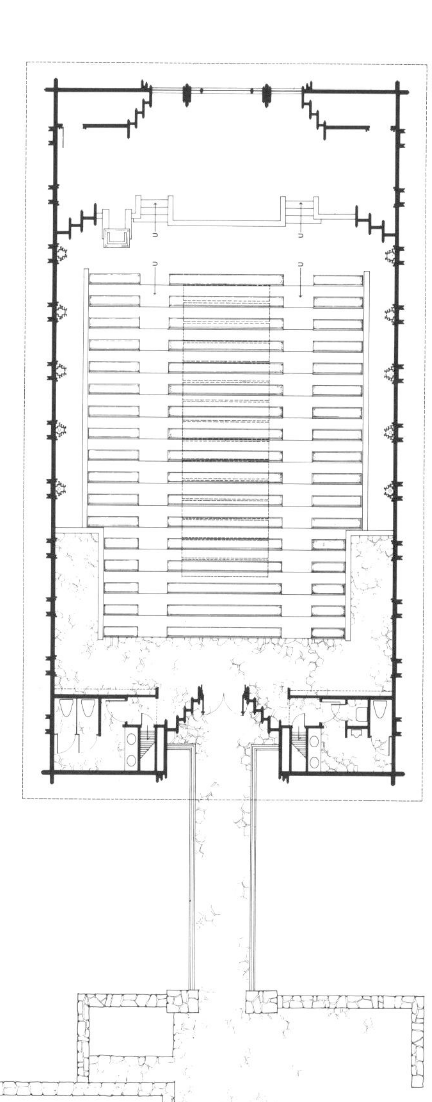

MILDRED B. COOPER MEMORIAL CHAPEL

Ornamentation is wrought in the warp and woof of the structure. It is constitutional in the best sense.

FRANK LLOYD WRIGHT
In the Cause of Architecture

As two Mozart sonatas may share a three-part musical framework yet vary in key and ultimately in kind, the Mildred B. Cooper Memorial Chapel explores, expands, and transposes the Gothic theme introduced at Thorncrown Chapel. Cooper Chapel, commissioned by the children of Mr. and Mrs. John Cooper, Sr., in honor of the late Mrs. Cooper, is set in a dense grove on a hill above the 7,000-person community of Bella Vista, Arkansas.

To visitors walking along the curved stone path among a forest of pines, the mass of the chapel looms like a tall Gothic gate. A storybook, steeply pitched gable roof extends low beyond the side walls, its overhangs supported by curved metal brackets. A wide Gothic arch pierces the redwood end wall and points to an oculus above, a round, unglazed window which seems shot through the screen wall as if by a bullet.

Inside, a deep Gothic arch, outlined like ship's framing with wood lathe, forms a high vestibule. Beyond the lowered entry, lyrically insistent arches spring upward into the sanctuary, where light and space achieve an unanticipated fullness.

Like Thorncrown, Cooper is one symmetrical room set on a rectangular stone platform between parallel stone walls. Wood laces Thorncrown's heart together, but, as Jones says, "Cooper Chapel is actually a steel building inside a wood building. Together they make a strong building."

Jones began with the concept of the Gothic arch, then, by pursuing the "operative opposite" principle, explored the tensile qualities of steel—its abilities to arch and soar. In thirteenth-century chapels, the characteristic stone flying buttresses supported heavy walls as they distributed forces to the earth, freed broad surfaces for stained glass, and were themselves ornamental. Cooper Chapel's interior Gothic arches form the structural bracing, obviating the need for buttresses. Bent steel I beams, painted a soft bronze hue, grip each other like interlocked fingers of opposite hands to collect and transfer weight and to open the building's walls to the forest's shifting chiaroscuro. Columns at six-foot intervals, a man-made forest, define the side walls.

Unlike the overriding transparency of Thorncrown, Cooper Chapel captures space more forcefully, cupping it within its delicate arches and holding it between the solid stone floor and well-defined end walls. But like Thorncrown, Cooper Chapel exults in light. The stained glass windows in Gothic chapels and cathedrals integrated illumination and storytelling; at Cooper Chapel

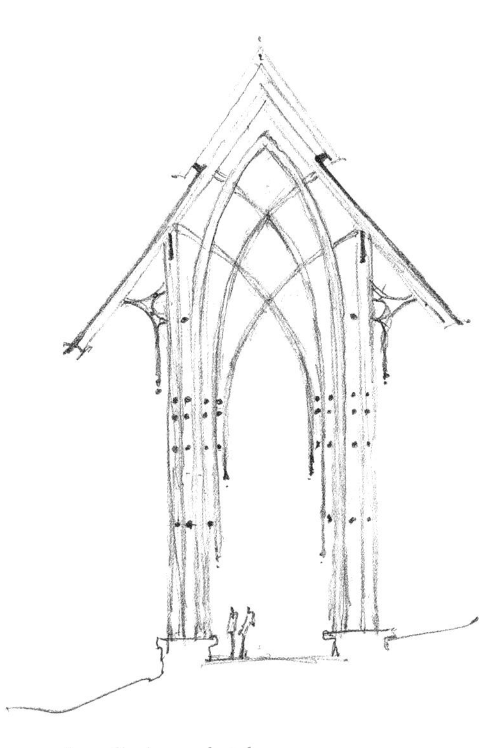

A preliminary sketch.

BELLA VISTA, ARKANSAS
1988

nature shines beyond the altar through clear windows, walls, and skylit roof. Jones, in his words, captured "an ever-changing array of light and shade."

By late afternoon, as the deep rose of an Arkansas sunset colors the windows, the space evolves. Floor-mounted indirect lamps and wall-mounted fixtures bathe the potlatch ceiling with incandescent warmth and render the view through glass walls more obscure. At dusk, the forest disappears behind smooth black walls. In an exchange of transparency for opacity, the building's volume emerges with the soft clarity of evening illumination.

In its massing, Cooper Chapel seems more solid than Thorncrown, yet its interior webbing is lighter and more delicate than that of its sibling. Thorncrown is reduced to essentials, sculptural and organic; Cooper is more architectonic and historically referential. There is music in both.

When asked to compare the beauty of the two chapels, John Williams, founder of the architecture school at the University of Arkansas, asked, "Which is more beautiful: a straight or a curved line?" Cooper Chapel's curving arches shape what Jones intended to be a musical offering, "an instrument that nature can play on."

The chapel rises within its Ozark setting above the community of Bella Vista, Arkansas. The entry wall offers protection and enclosure, while side walls of wood and glass open up the building.

Left: Wood columns at six foot intervals rest on stone walls. Paired metal brackets spring from the columns to the underside of broadly overhanging eaves. The building displays both the taut energy of steel and the strength of wood.

Right: Shadows play on the arched entry area's wood lathe and create an Oriental tranquillity.

Opposite: Front elevation. A rose window cuts through the wall above a large Gothic arch. Framing splays wider as it ascends above the doorway.

Below: Section looking toward the altar. Steel arches continue above the window to the underside of the roof.

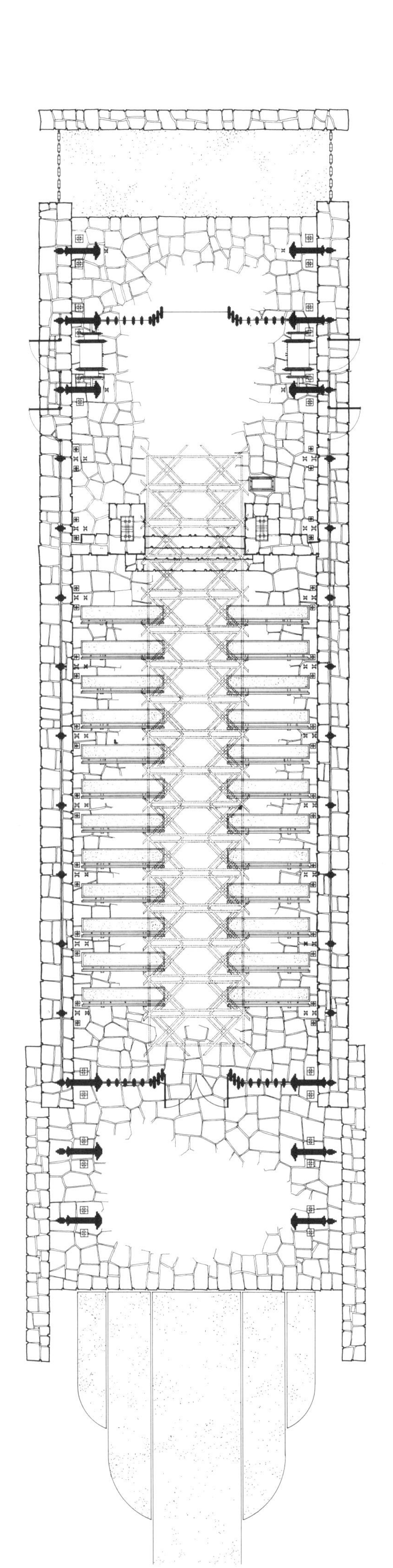

Left: Floor plan. A straight stone platform and side walls cradle the curvilinear superstructure.

Below: Metal door handles on a scored oak doorway.

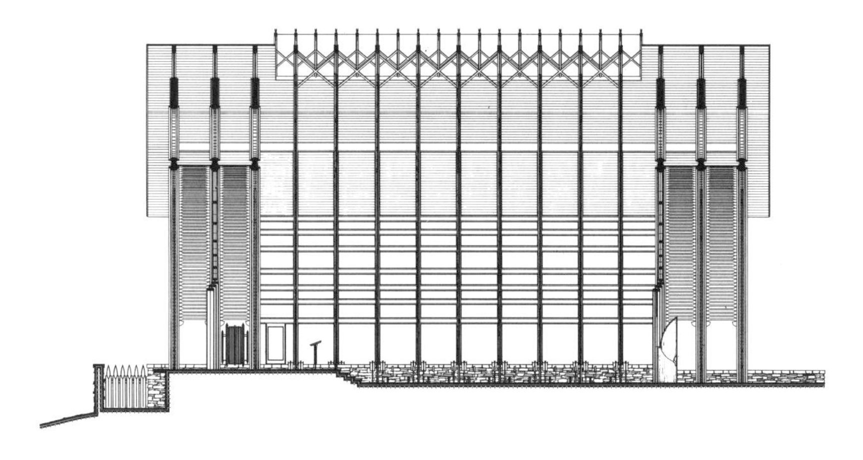

Opposite, above: Abstract patterns in structure, seen from beneath. The chapel interior's exuberant metal construction reveals Jones's training in engineering, and is reminiscent of such nineteenth-century masters in metal as Gustave Eiffel and Joseph Paxton. Jones's characteristic cross-shaped bracing in wood and curving steel redefines the term "organic" architecture, in which structural necessity and ornamental effect combine. The result is characteristic of Jones alone.

The longitudinal section shows how the beginning and end of an otherwise transparent chapel are strongly defined.

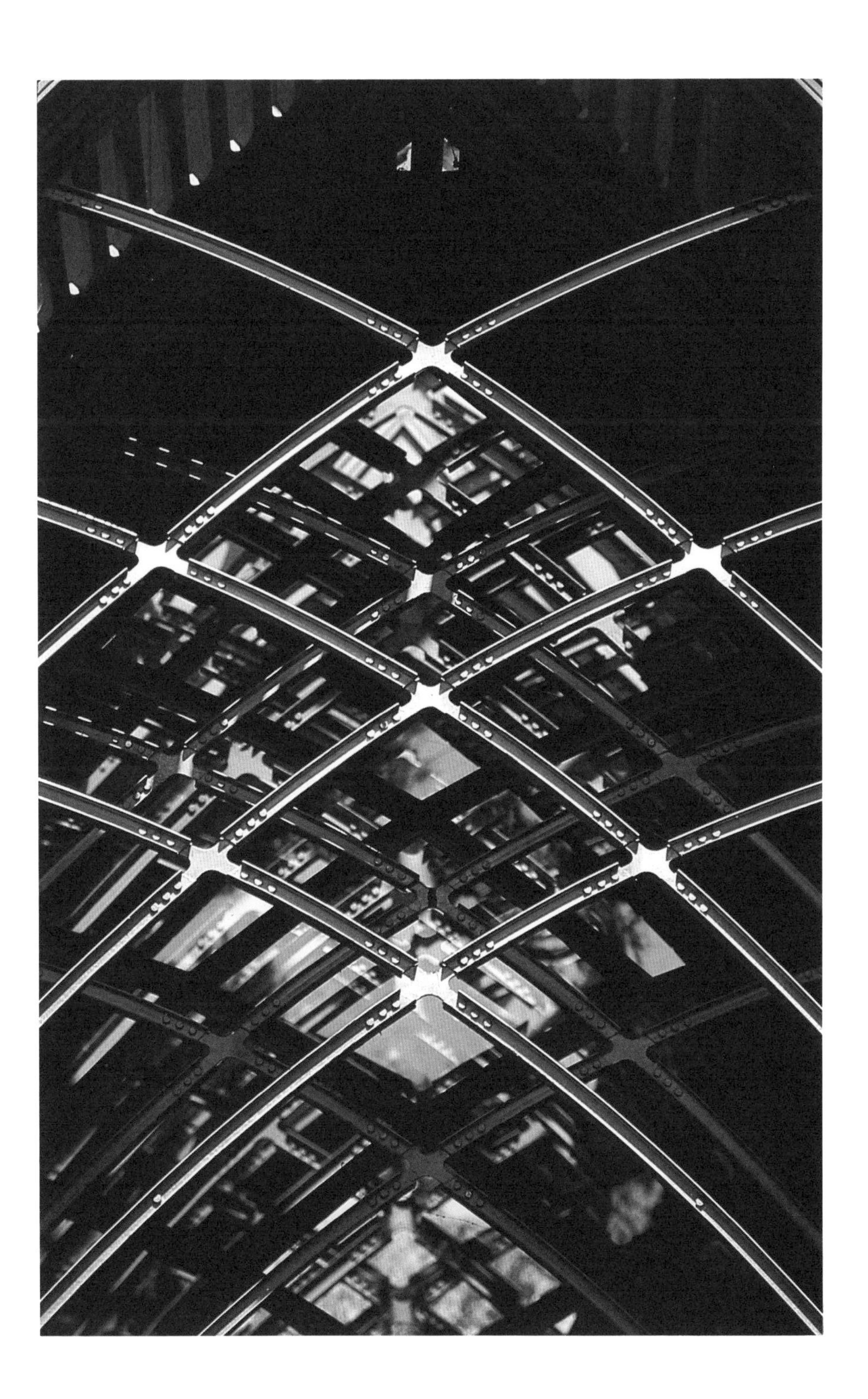

A custom metal grate above a recessed light fixture inset into stonework.

Broad roof overhangs, solid redwood walls, and a steel heart combine into what Jones calls a "strong" building.

MARTY LEONARD COMMUNITY CHAPEL

Opposite: In the choir loft, milled wood walls contribute to verticality.

"Sanctuary" means both a place of worship and a place of refuge. The Marty Leonard Community Chapel provides sanctuary for the inhabitants of Fort Worth's Lena Pope Home, a residential treatment center for emotionally disturbed adolescents. In its mission statement, the chapel is described as "a serene setting where the youth. . . can give and receive acceptance and understanding. . . a peaceful place where the youth can let down their walls . . . an uplifting environment that inspires people."

Jones received the chapel commission at the request of Fort Worth resident and board member Marty Leonard. When she received the seed money for the construction of a chapel as a fiftieth birthday present from family and friends, she had not met Jones but had seen photographs of Thorncrown Chapel, which inspired her. She consequently spearheaded a private fund-raising effort that culminated in the chapel's dedication in November 1990. The chapel is a gift to the Lena Pope Home from the private community.

Gothic archetype, favored by Ruskin and Wright, inspired this building meant to inspire others. The new brick-and-wood chapel embodies the solid authority of its spiritual ancestors and shares their ability to cradle and protect, to stimulate the emotions, and to transcend experience. It is Jones's most substantial ecclesiastical work to date.

The chapel is placed not in the quiet Ozark woods but on a bare Texas hill outside Fort Worth next to Interstate 30. Related to both the rolling brown landscape and to the Lena Pope Home's low-scaled buildings, the chapel is separated from nearby buff-colored residential units and from the highway by a low-walled open courtyard.

From the courtyard, the earth-colored building stands tall, erect, and thin, while it "sails out toward the freeway like a clipper ship," in the words of architecture critic David Dillon of the *Dallas Morning News.* Its blocky base rises to staggered shake roofs set above high walls in an active, unfolding form that gives no hint of the interior's complex spatial character, its forceful mass, or its contemplative qualities.

This 3,000-square-foot chapel seats only 150 people in twenty-eight pews yet commands the unquestioned authority of a small cathedral. Jones's control of scale is masterful: stout brick columns, cruciform in section, express vertical structure; broad structural wood pilasters support hefty wooden beams that span the nave; pendent lanterns punctuate the open height.

LENA POPE HOME
FORT WORTH, TEXAS
1990

Opposite: In the nave, a large braced window beyond the altar steps out toward the highway. Masonry columns, wood framing and walls, and the scale of the structure contribute to its spatial density.

Left: View across transept, showing ample wood beams, which lower truss height at the crossing.

Below: Longitudinal section of the chapel, which rises to sixty feet. Its complex spatial blend includes high vestibule, lower choir loft/mezzanine, and high nave. The wide altar and deep transept extend the volume outward.

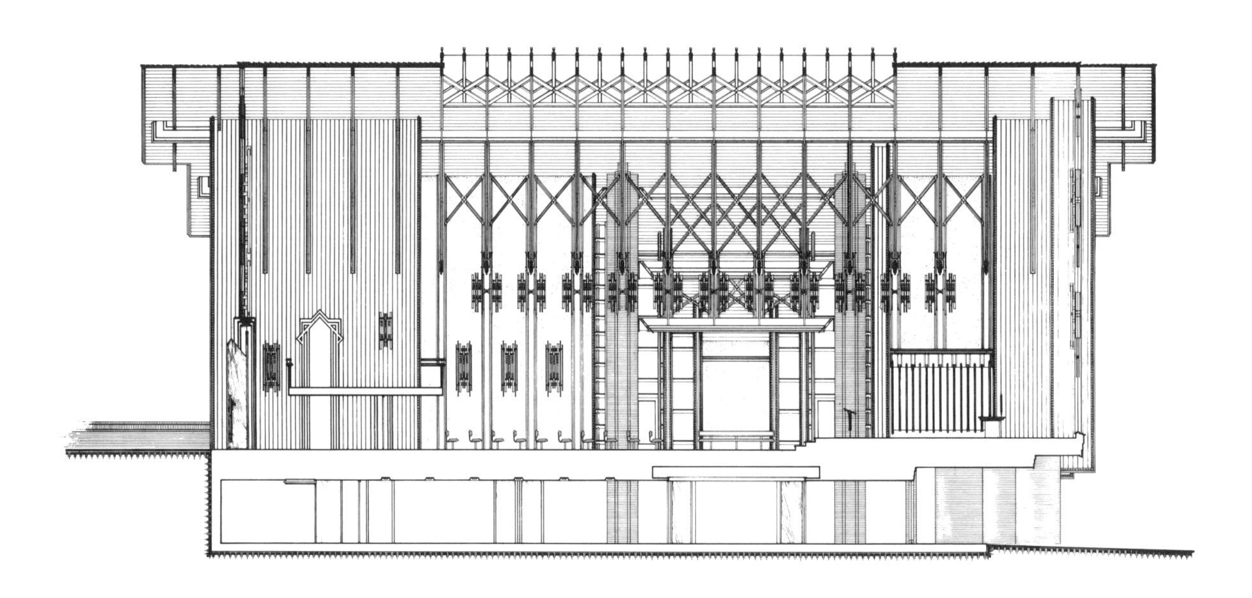

The plan is cruciform—vestibule, nave, transept, and chancel. Interior space expands upward and laterally from the narrow vestibule to its widest point at the transept, achieving a depth that exceeds the interior's nominal dimensions.

As stained glass filters sunlight into Gothic churches, the windows in this chapel filter sunlight through structure. From lanterns to beams to superimposed bracing to ridgetop skylight, the Leonard chapel weaves a net of light. The eye is drawn upward to the fulsome space above the cross-nave beam line and its interconnected tissue of diagonal wood and metal bracing.

Light beige walls, brownish-buff brick flooring, and light gray Philippine mahogany warm the nave. Metal bracing and bracketing, structural saddles, and incidental pieces, all painted light bronze, imply the permanence of Gothic stonework without stone's mass. Vertically applied milled wood covers several interior walls (and the exterior). As in Jones's other ecclesiastical commissions, the architect designed all incidental pieces, from desks to wastepaper baskets, pews, lanterns, and lecterns.

Opaque side walls block the interstate highway's distractions and focus the worshipers' attention on the fifty-foot-tall altar window. To one seated in the pews, the view is of clouds and sky; only when standing does the reality of the highway intrude. Like the sanctuary's entry wall, the altar window's massive scale is broken by Jones's characteristic wood bracing, its ridges outlined and underscored by bronze metal.

This building, highly visible from the interstate, has made the Pope Home well known throughout Tarrant County, and the home's board has opened the chapel to the larger Fort Worth community. Like Thorncrown, the Leonard Chapel may become a pilgrimage destination, since the eccentric facades intrigue passersby and promise inner mysteries. Within, the chapel soars toward an inner serenity while providing what its builders sought for their young charges—"peace and a new beginning." ▲

Opposite: Wood and metal composite trusses inhabit a separate space high above the floor and contribute to an allusive murkiness.

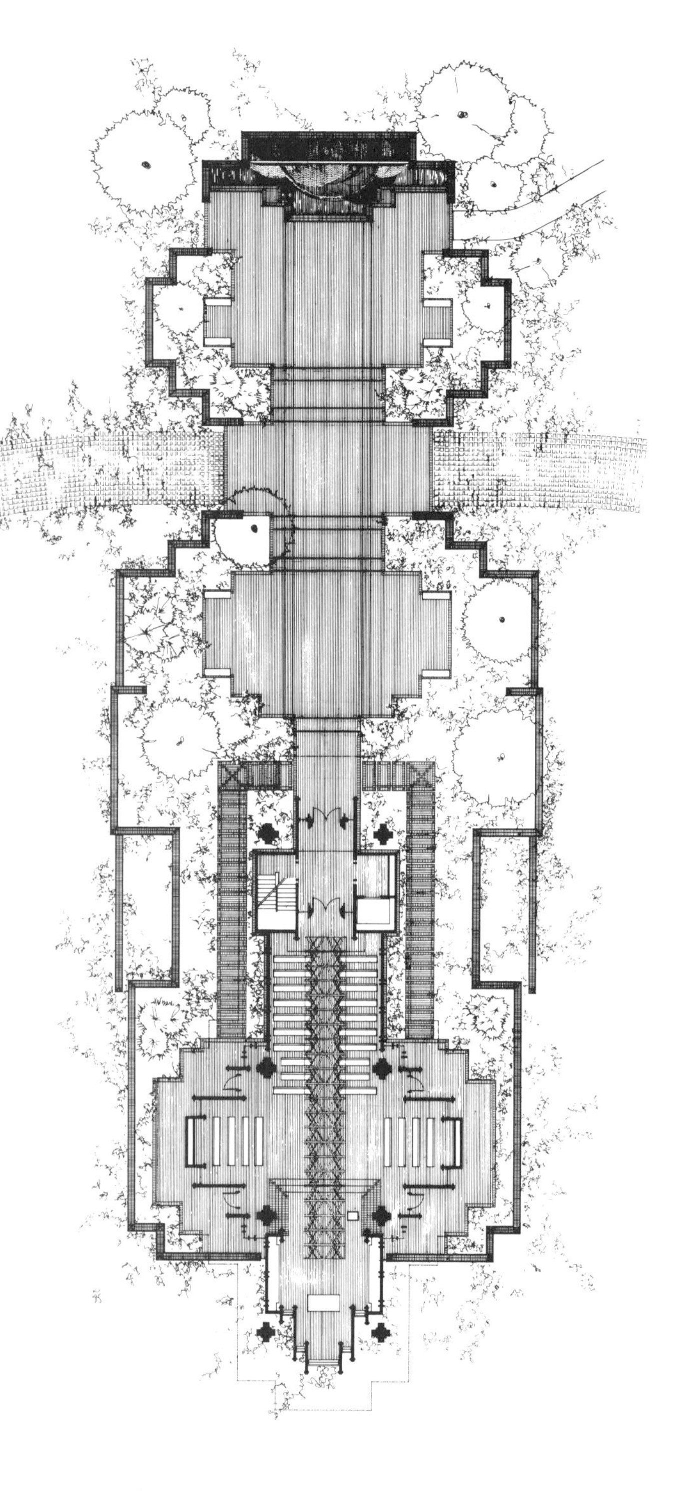

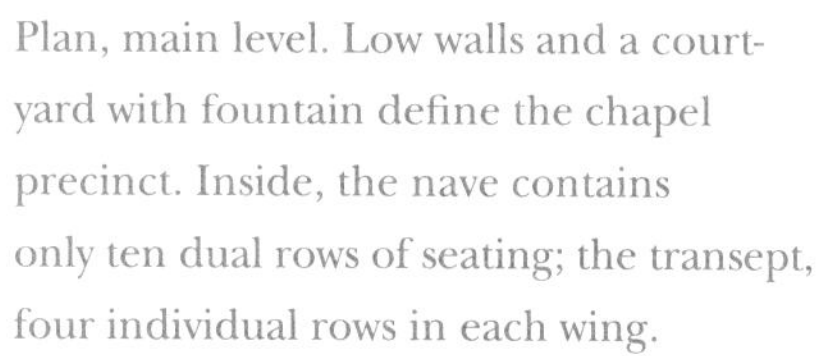

Plan, main level. Low walls and a courtyard with fountain define the chapel precinct. Inside, the nave contains only ten dual rows of seating; the transept, four individual rows in each wing.

Opposite: Staggered shake roof, which drops at the transept and steps upward. Layered walls follow a cruciform plan, masking direct sunlight while opening to the sides.

Buff-colored courtyard walls relate the building to low-scaled brick structures on this residential campus and match Fort Worth's winter landscape.

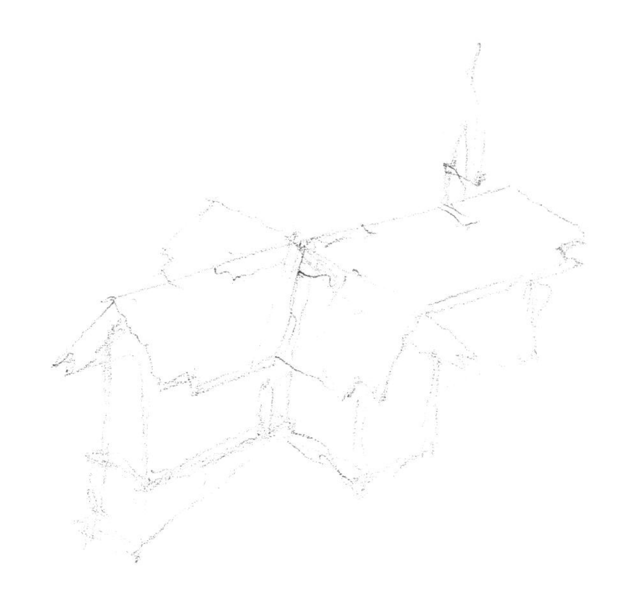

Above: Early sketch showing transept. Jones explores ideas through plan, section, and elevation sketches and in simple axonometric drawings. Larger models and on-site visits refine three-dimensional ideas.

Left: Entry elevation from courtyard. Though construction of the chapel began in 1989, a tornado blew off part of the roof of the building as it neared completion in April 1990 and caused some internal damage. Additional supporting structural members were subsequently added.

Right: Metal door handles correspond to a steep roof. Southern light casts strong shadows on wood doors scored with a large X motif that typifies the Leonard Chapel's window framing.

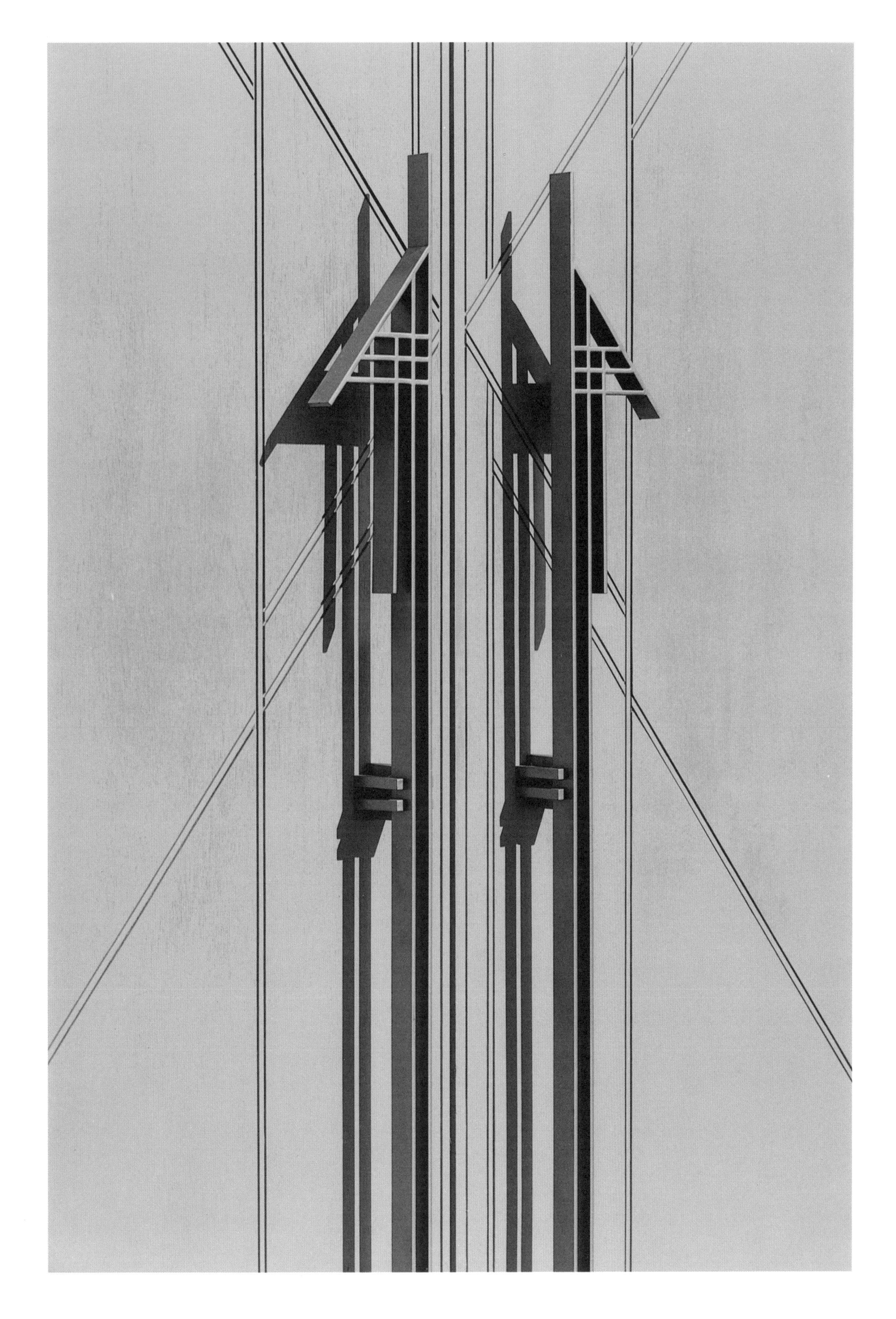

Pinecote Pavilion hovers within its forest setting like a wildfowl beside a pond. Clearly a built object, this simple shed responds to its setting so strongly that comparisons of building to nature seem inevitable. Like a woodland creature, the pavilion strikes no aggressive pose; instead, it blends with the pines and grasses, shadows and light—alert and at peace with its surroundings.

The pavilion, a masterwork that rivals Thorncrown Chapel, was designed for the Crosby Arboretum, a 1,600-acre complex dedicated to the "interaction of naturally occurring species." It is critically placed as the first of several buildings planned for the arboretum's 64-acre native plant center near Picayune, Mississippi. It lies near the heart of the arboretum's collection of eleven distinct environmental systems representing areas scattered throughout southwestern Mississippi.

People and nature meet under the folded roof, where music is played, slides are shown in the evenings, and visitors congregate, sheltered from subtropical sun and rain. Walks through a pine savanna, which has evolved on the site of a former strawberry field, begin at the pavilion. Eventually, it will be joined by an exhibition space, an office building, and a maintenance building.

A remarkable unity of design unfolds along the paths circling the pavilion. Small and large details cohere into one integrated work carefully melded with the site design, which was initially planned by consultants including Philadelphia's Andropogon Associates and coordinated by landscape architect Edward Blake. Clues to the larger framework can be seen in individual fragments: sculptural metal gates, fabricated near Jones's home in Arkansas; a water fountain that evokes Mesoamerican forms; a diminutive, assertive weir that draws a line between two levels of pond water as it steps downward, bringing movement and sound; and smooth bench seating on wooden bridges. All these elements refer to a theme fully explored at the pavilion.

Viewed from a distance, the open building seems to float on a pond, recalling the spirit of the Kinkakuji, the Golden Pavilion at Kyoto, and encouraging reflection on humanity's relationship with nature. Lightness and transparency underscore the waterside tranquillity, only slightly marred by an unseen, thundering interstate highway nearby.

As the path winds landward, the sculptural building's roof form dominates the approach, rising from short columns near the ground, widening in a stepped geometric progression into a strong

PICAYUNE, MISSISSIPPI
1987

The pavilion glows in south Mississippi's evening light.

folded form. Like the feathered wing of a bird, the roof is enriched by layering. From beams to joists to purlins to thick shingles, the roof rises, fills out, and evanesces into treillage and skylight at the edges.

Within, a strong space both enfolds and soars. Shadows move across the floor as they respond to the tall pines bending in the wind. Walls open out to the grasses or to the pond beyond. The line between "out" and "in" is blurred; the feeling is of finding shelter within the out-of-doors.

As in all of Jones's buildings, interior details reinforce total unity. Slender columns with high angular bracing reflect the branching of the longleaf pines outside. The floor sets up a rectangular grid, which is repeated in numerous details. Lamps (strong, sculptural forms that anchor the pavilion's four corners) and indirect lighting (inset within the floor, protected by custom-designed metal grids) all combine to form one glowing work in the evening landscape.

Materials harmonize with the surroundings. From wood that already has weathered to a greenish-gray, to earth-colored brick flooring that stretches beyond the shelter of the roofline into the open air, to wooden dowels and earth-toned metal connections, the colors and textures subtly blend with the environment while enriching the building.

The pavilion's greatest beauty lies in its bones. Pinecote is reticulated—its structural framework forms a unified network like that of a burned leaf. Column bracing illustrates the principle. These beams, which tie the building together laterally, ascend continuously from near ground level to an apex near the ceiling. Their repetition sets up a rhythm; seen in perspective, their receding, crossed-X forms reinforce the roof's height. The geometric metal ring joining the beams snaps the composition into focus. Like Gothic buttressing, Pinecote's simple columns and beams delight the eye while carrying their loads.

No cathedral, the pavilion is a secular variation on a theme Jones has explored in other work, though Pinecote is more modest —an open platform and roof that will receive myriad uses in its lifetime. Its assurance comes from being firmly rooted in its pine forest home. One small, woodland building set between earth, water, and sky, Pinecote pavilion brings nature's elements within touch.

Opposite: Like a Japanese landscape, elements merge within an ecologically sensitive setting.

The building's shed roof thins as it steps outward, from cedar shakes to exposed structure.

Gravel walks and bridges connect into a looping walkway on this 64-acre site.

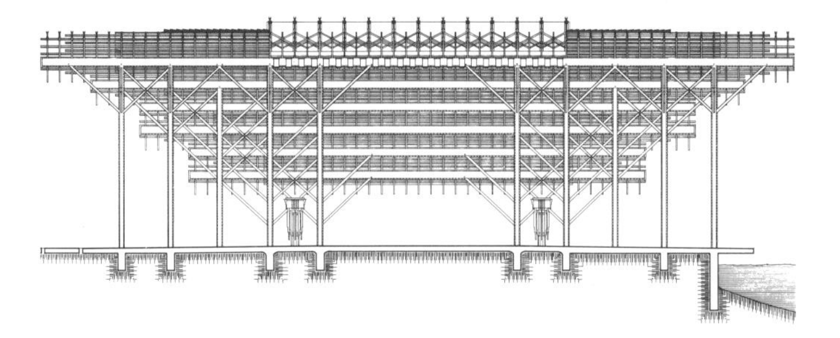

The pavilion's footprint, revealing a four-foot-by-six-foot grid of brick and wood. The building platform extends beyond the land into a dammed pond.

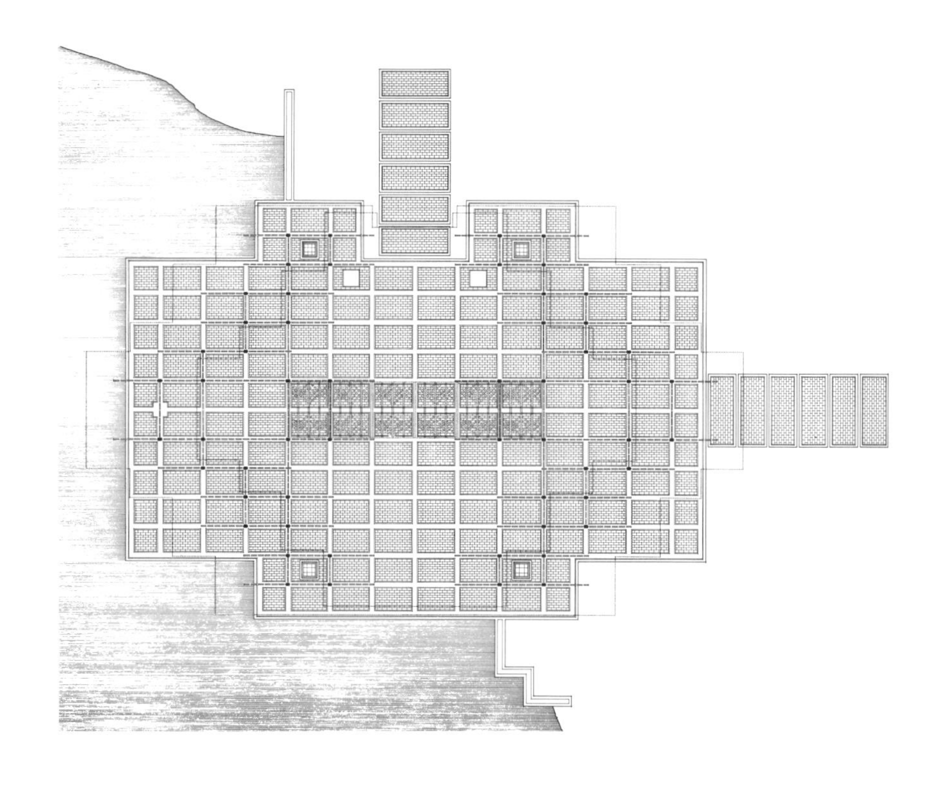

Opposite: Pinecote is low and wide in response to southern Mississippi's flat landscape. Columns supporting a 27-foot high roof resemble the surrounding pine forest.

Wood bridge and sloped wooden benches that serve as both barriers and resting places.

A man-made forest of notched columns which reflect natural texture and scale, fills the pavilion's interior.

Bench seating inside the pavilion sets interior boundaries. Metal is typically painted soft bronze.

According to Jones, the pine structure "is an assembly of many small pieces fastened together with nails, dowels, and metal connectors. There is complete exposure of each construction element, all visible from within and without."

Right: An exposed trellis recalls the work of earlier architects such as Greene and Greene and Bernard Maybeck.

View through the pavilion from the north entry out to lake. Continuous bracing traces the roofline, culminating in a skylight at the apex.

The pavilion's sculptural metal lanterns
paint with light.

Jones describes the small pavilion as both a simple gathering place in the landscape and as a more complex essay in "the poetics of revealed construction."

Small but powerful Pine Eagle chapel punctuates the tree-rimmed lake at Camp Tiak, near Wiggins, Mississippi, capturing the spiritual qualities of transcendence and imminence in its frame. The structure both points upward—aligning itself with universal, timeless forces—and opens outward—framing the immediate world like a Zen window.

Although directly related to Oriental models, such as the ascending, multiple roofs and placement beside a still pond of Japan's Golden Pavilion, Pine Eagle chapel reflects other influences. In elevation and in cross-bracing the building recalls the abstract geometric patterning and elemental forms of native American design. Echoes of the American barn and the Gothic cathedral are combined in a single, forceful mélange that is entirely new and intended for one specific place.

The place is a Boy Scout camp in a south Mississippi pine wilderness. The waterborne chapel, located on a dock structure beside a small lake, inhabits a circumscribed world. Intended to serve various needs from daily chapel to camp lectures and occasional musicales, the structure demonstrates its kinship with Pinecote Pavilion at the Crosby Arboretum. Both were gifts of south Mississippi's L. O. Crosby, Jr., family, many of whom have been active in scouting.

Compared with Pinecote, Pine Eagle is tiny. So much is compressed in such a small space: 500 square feet versus Pinecote's 5000, yet its 25-foot height approaches Pinecote's. The exaggerated height of Pine Eagle's layered roofs, filled with an abundance of Jones's characteristic cross-bracing, exhibits a controlled mannerism. The thick woven network of diagonal wood, junctures marked with a multiplicity of hollow steel connecting rings, adds the illusion of mass to the shed while allowing it to remain transparent.

Strict geometry, in 32-inch repetition, orders the composition. All significant structural members, from southern yellow pine columns to rafters to standing seam copper roofs (on regular half-modules of 16 inches), follow the pattern. The roofs both lengthen (in the long dimension) and compress (as they rise) according to regulated pattern. The consistent repetition establishes a rhythm within the constricted envelope of the structure.

Symmetrical storage rooms anchor and protect the ground level, but captured space is not at issue. Former Eagle Scout Jones has embraced the natural fullness of the surroundings as an open-air temple. Eighty people can be seated on simple pine benches under the trees for rituals and ceremonies, and no roof blocks the clouds.

What can architecture contribute? What is its purpose? It is hoped that this small structure will provide a strong and appropriate setting—a backdrop and silhouette—for the rituals and ceremonies that will take place here in the years to come.

Architecturally, this small pavilion—small in size, but large in purpose and spirit—attempts to align itself with the earth, the water, and the sky . . . with the wonderful bounties of nature.

It is hoped that, if the architecture aligns itself with these natural features—which are the clearest manifestations of some higher order in the universe—perhaps it can in some contributing way (as model, as symbol) invite and inspire those who come to use it to align themselves, in more beneficial and meaningful ways, with the natural forces of life.

The degree to which it fulfills that purpose will be the final measure of its success. It is now ready for that test.

FAY JONES
DEDICATION SPEECH
NOVEMBER 24, 1991

CAMP TIAK
WIGGINS, MISSISSIPPI
1991

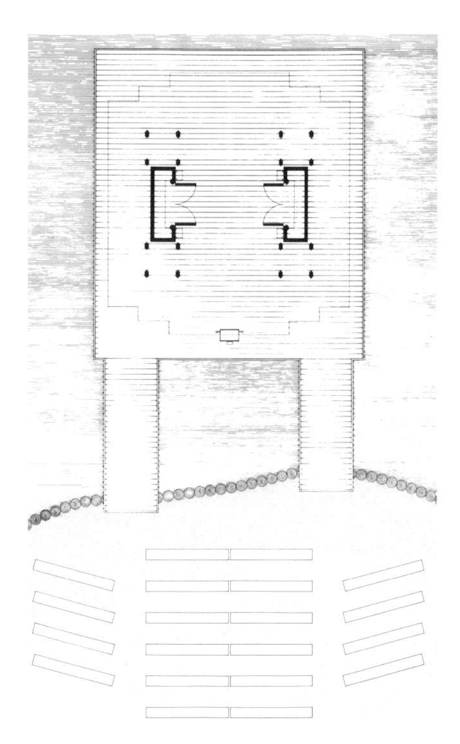
The interfaith chapel rests on a lakeside dock connected to land by twin gangways.

The chapel opens directly onto the lake, where surrounding pines are reflected in black water.

By including forest, lake, and sky in his composition and making the structure a natural complement to these natural features rather than an intrusion, Jones has made the chapel open, like a window, to a larger world. Symbolic language is almost audible through Pine Eagle's transparent, visceral grasp: "Here! Now!"

Dense cross-bracing fills the area beneath ascending roofs, adding mass to the tiny pavilion. Kiln-dried southern yellow pine and a copper battened seam roof are the chapel's primary building materials.

RESIDENCES

Opposite: Screened from the street, the Jones residence is set on a suburban hillside in north Fayetteville. Curving stone walls announce the drive.

Although the residence shares certain characteristics with other contemporary buildings of the mid-fifties, a strong individualism textures the exterior. Redwood siding, stone, and glass coexist on the east elevation.

FAYETTEVILLE, ARKANSAS
1955

Fay Jones's first building was like a spring. When tapped, a lifetime's welled-up expectations, experience, training, and ideals flowed into one project. The small building distills a broad spectrum of the architect's design principles, from structure to philosophy. The Jones family has called the experiment their home since it was completed in May 1956.

There is still excitement in his voice as Jones tells the story of the design and building of his house. In 1955, when a young local developer sought plans for speculative houses in north Fayetteville, Jones saw a chance for his family to acquire a home. "I had been teaching a couple of years. We had been living in a spec house a few blocks away. It was an opportunity to be a bona fide architect, to test the water. [The builder] thought that a better designed house ought to be worth more."

Creative financing helped set the architect's fee for the house he was to design for his family. "If I buy it, don't pay me a fee; if you sell it, pay me a fee," he offered. Although initial estimates set the cost at an affordable $12,500, an unforeseen boulder unearthed during construction pushed the price upward. Several months after moving day (May 1956), the assistant professor and his wife obtained 100 percent financing from the local savings and loan association. The $15,000 they borrowed represented only 60 percent of the building's newly appraised value of $25,000. "The theory really worked. Design counts for something," Jones says.

He was prepared for the commission, having "thought-built" the house over a period of years. "I had been looking forward to a house, doodling with theoretical ideas, waiting around for a specific site," he recalls. It took only one long weekend to get construction underway.

At the time, the Joneses' property was one of the northernmost building sites in Fayetteville. The 70-by-140-foot lot, which drops steeply to the north and east, faces west, typical of sloping lots throughout Arkansas. A lake lay at the foot of the east slope; the forested hillside above it created a natural draw, a funnel for cool air movement up the slope to the building site.

The architect planned a house with two levels to provide separate recreational space for the couple's two daughters, who had discovered rock 'n' roll. Jones set the upper floor, dedicated to adult living, dining, and sleeping, in the treetops. The ground level, nestled against the hillside, was for the children, for the architect's studio, and for cars.

Every man should have a place where he can have communion with himself and his surroundings, a personal environment free from disharmony and frustrations: a place to nurture his ideals and aspirations. That place should be his home and if it transcends mere building and becomes a work of art it is architecture.

FAY JONES

The Joneses' house clarified the architect's residential design approach of providing pragmatic, private houses, concerned not primarily with image but with living. Mated with the hillside and reaching into space, this house introduced the theme of harmony with nature that has dominated subsequent projects.

Wood and stone, which reappear many times in the architect's work, are appropriate to this site. Set back from a suburban street past curving stone walls, the reticent west elevation shields family activities from passersby. There is no apparent front door leading into the horizontal, modernist composition. An exploratory sequence accompanies entry from street approach to hearthside. One enters underneath the structure, where a path invites the visitor through the covered carport toward the trees. An abrupt right turn in the open pathway leads to the entry door. The floor of the overhead deck shelters the walkway from the rain.

The ground floor is strong, cavelike, and reminiscent of Bruce Goff's houses. The vestibule, dark and cool, has lowered ceilings and stone floors. To the left, space flows into a greenhouse filled with flowering impatiens and ferns; overhead lights are softened by translucent fiberglass panels. The conservatory space turns a corner to what seems to be out-of-doors.

Adjusting to the light, one's eye focuses on the exposed boulder that forms the ground floor's south wall. Maidenhair fern and moss cover its damp flank; water drips down the boulder's face into a free-form pool. Cool light from the conservatory spills across the stone; stalactite-like lamps throw the wall's further recesses into relief. The view from Jones's desk extends through rocky shadows toward the conservatory and through the screened door to the green outdoors. "For years, my front-end work, the conceptual phase, was done there," he says.

Opposite: The covered walkway to the main entrance passes under the outdoor deck and by the daughters' bedroom.

If the first level suggests compression, the top of the staircase brings an exuberant release. A light, open living space replaces the lower level's shadows, its drama heightened by contrast. Daylight is everywhere, its presence heightened by a minimal number of interior walls. The ceiling pitches upward into a high gable, and glass walls surrounding the space blur the distinction between open air and heated space. Seemingly anchored by a massive, stepped stone chimney in one corner, the room hangs lightly in the treetops.

Space flows from the sitting area around the fireplace into the glass-walled dining area with its adjacent deck facing north. No high wall separates the sleeping area at the south end of the

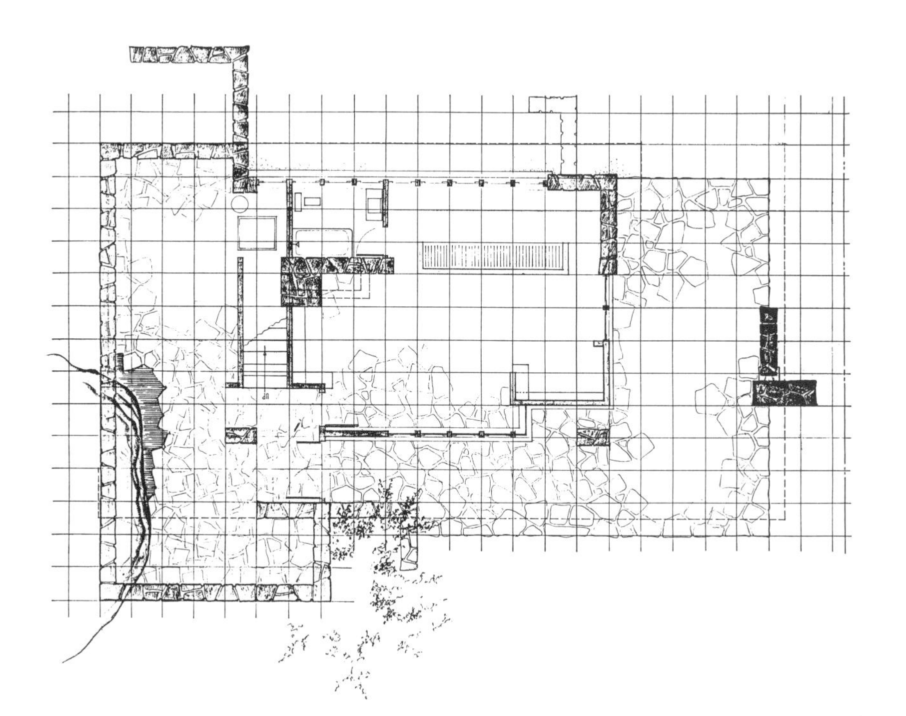

Plan, lower level. Jones arrived at the foundation scheme quickly, but modified his plan when construction unearthed a large boulder. His studio, the site of much "front-end work, conceptual work," showing stones laid as he found them near a creek bed. Natural light enters through a skylit conservatory.

building from the larger whole. The south wall consists of undraped jalousy windows opening to an ivy-covered retaining wall; all other windows open to the trees. Only the bathrooms have doors.

Although the dramatic interior volume suggests a large floor area, the living room's dimensions are actually 11 by 17 feet and the contiguous dining area is only 8 by 14 feet. Despite an absence of corridors and interior walls, juxtaposition of spaces allows proximity with privacy. The long galley kitchen adjacent to the living and dining spaces is separated from them by a low wall, allowing easy conversation between spaces with some visual privacy during meal preparation.

For Fay Jones, a new house required new furniture. "When the house was complete, Fay said, 'We're leaving the furniture behind,'" says Gus Jones. "Fay was right, of course, because we had to be consistent with his ideas, and this was not only sensible, but typical of Fay's thinking." Her understanding was strained, however, when her husband cut off the legs of newly purchased living room chairs.

Like a true Wright disciple, Jones designed most of the other interior furnishings. Simplicity distinguishes the long, low dining table, a pragmatic hallmark of all of Jones's subsequent work: a plywood door with a pumpkin-colored plastic laminate top forms the tabletop; the accompanying stools, hollow plywood boxes with lift-off lids, cost $4 each when constructed at a local cabinet shop.

Explaining the visible structural systems that undergird and ornament his residence, Jones says, "My strong concern is how the structure works." Unlike much of Wright's work, in which internal structural systems are concealed, Jones's house tells the story of its making in its members. It is a "long beam" house, harking back to early Scandinavian or Japanese wood building traditions in which interior structural beams continue fully expressed through the exterior of a building. Three beams, two on the opposing interior walls and one asymmetrically placed off the gable's peak, line the ceiling to clearly express their structural roles.

Jones says he knew that "in a house this open, you need something for longitudinal, horizontal bracing," so he designed a strong chimney to support longitudinal structural members and to build what Wright referred to as the psychological "heart center" of the house. Jones helped lay the chimney's stonework and personalized the lintel by scratching a distinctive texture into wet concrete with a nail-studded stick. Custom steel fireside implements, forged in a local shop, carry Jones's distinctive design signature as well.

The range of materials employed in the house is compatible and limited: fieldstone for foundation walls, columns, and the fireplace; fir for paneling and cabinets; and sheet glass 7/32-inch thick (not plate glass) for windows. Outdoors, materials are more varied: rough-sawn redwood siding, roofing shingles, concrete deck topping, corrugated steel for the lower exterior soffit, and sliding aluminum windows. In retrospect, Jones says he would have narrowed his choices outside to fewer materials. There is, however, a textural richness in their profusion.

Contrasting surfaces invite touch, including soft carpet, hard stone, smooth wood, and slick glass. Pleasant odors emanate from fireside woodsmoke and damp stone. Water dripping into a hidden pond and wind moving through the trees produce unexpected sounds. Colors range from drab to brilliant in an intentional sequence from soft natural colors outside the building to the warm colors of hearthside pillows.

The interior is bathed with both artificial and natural light for controlled effect. Windows line the exterior walls, their size dependent on orientation and their rhythm governed by the 32-inch module that frames them. Kite-shaped windows help destroy potentially dead space at the high corners of the gables by bringing what Jones calls "a high delineating light."

All artificial lighting sources are hidden. Light filtering up from wide interior soffits visually extends the interior's depth and height. A continuous band of downlights, made of materials left over from edging a handrail, line a seating cove. Individual ceiling fixtures contain incandescent bulbs in simple ceramic fixtures protected by patterned wood baffles.

The open plan, with built-in furniture and low walls, creates generous spaces. The east wall, open for light and cooling, is set on a thirty-two inch grid. Service spaces line the west wall and the deck serves as a sleeping porch.

Jones uses mirrors to catch light and play tricks with space. Diamond-shaped mirrors underneath windows in the high gables fool the eye; mirrors placed in thin vertical strips melt corners and expand space. "There is something magical about illusions . . . a pause, a visual interest," says Jones.

Wit, warmth, and energy characterize the Jones residence. Edward Durell Stone commented on its contained energy when he stated that it "looks like the inside of a piano." But the highest compliment came from Frank Lloyd Wright, who visited the house a year before his death. As he walked up the narrow staircase and turned to admire the main living space, he smiled at his former apprentice and said, "Fay, I am going to have to give you a certificate." In a subsequent lecture at the University of Arkansas,

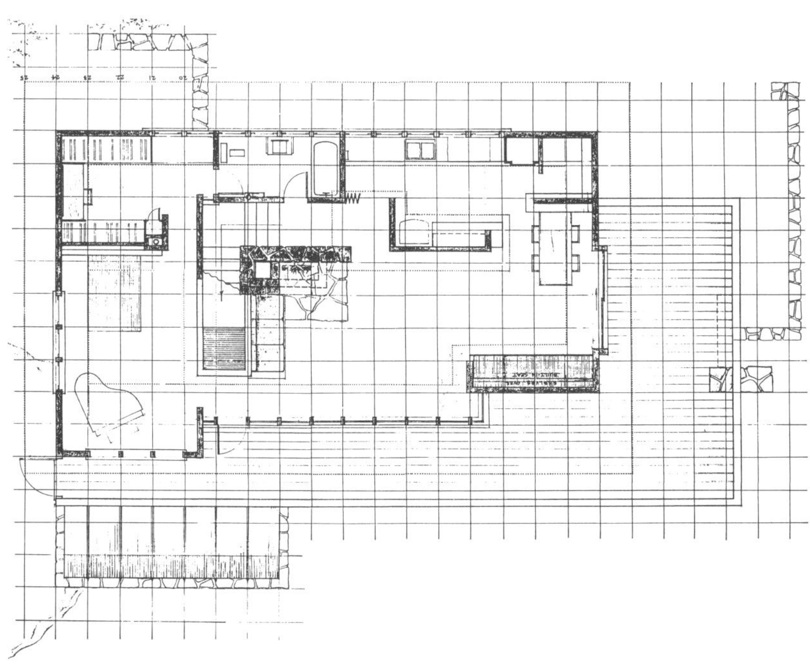

Wright invited members of the audience to visit Jones's house as an example of organic architecture. People still seek it out.

The significance of Jones's earliest building lies in the completeness of its expression, an expression of innate modesty and vitality—qualities of its maker. While later residences would refine Jones's expression of the organic building principles first stated here, none would more fully declare his ambitions.

When the Joneses built their house in 1955–56, it was "the farthest one north" in Fayetteville. Today, the building is unchanged, though the town has surrounded it. The generous, open residence is actually Jones's second treehouse: his first was built as a boy in El Dorado. The house's deck skims above a cavelike lower level.

PINE KNOLL

LITTLE ROCK, ARKANSAS
1964

Northeast corner. Finely laid native limestone rises in horizontal bands.

Three hours and the Ozark mountains separate Little Rock from Fayetteville, Arkansas. Fay Jones had misgivings about working there: "I had never built a house this far from home. I felt that I could only visit the building site once or twice a week." Desire for an important commission overcame his doubts; instead, his concern prompted careful planning and more than 100 sheets of working drawings for a superbly crafted contemporary estate known as Pine Knoll.

Perspective drawing of north, or river, elevation.

Pine Knoll is a subtle, studied essay, the result of shared intent. When career diplomat Graham Hall retired from foreign service in India and Australia to return to his native Little Rock, he and his wife considered moving to a large family home nearby. Instead, they chose to build a new house on a bluff overlooking the Arkansas River. Their taste and insight informed and enriched the building to an unusual extent.

The wooded site they chose had a view south across the river, just downstream from the spot where Mr. and Mrs. Hall had become engaged. At their request, the architect had a temporary fourteen-foot-high hillside platform built prior to construction to confirm the view. Hall and his wife followed the entire construction process from a rented house nearby.

Adhering to a Wrightian principle that a house should not sit on, but just over, a hill's crest, Pine Knoll's main story nestles along the length of a river bluff. A small lawn, carved from the surrounding deciduous forest, crowns the hilltop. Just below the lawn, a long, low roof dominates the south elevation. The house unfolds in modulated layers as the hill drops toward the river.

What seems to be a single-story house actually contains a second level. When approached from the drive or the garden, the roof gradually yields to columns and windows; through the house, where outdoor deck meets window, the wall evanesces to light and air. From the river side, the main floor hangs over the lower one to form a rhythmic stone arcade—a covered porch that shelters guest bedrooms.

Smaller buildings extend the composition into the landscape much as did the dependencies of nineteenth-century houses. Mr. Hall, who raised and raced pigeons, requested a dovecote nearby. From his perch above the dovecote, he awaited the daily return of his flock to the Orientally inspired, hipped-roof structure. The current owners have converted the dovecote into a playhouse for grandchildren, but they have retained the original use of another outbuilding, a quiet greenhouse marked by a custom-designed wood trellis.

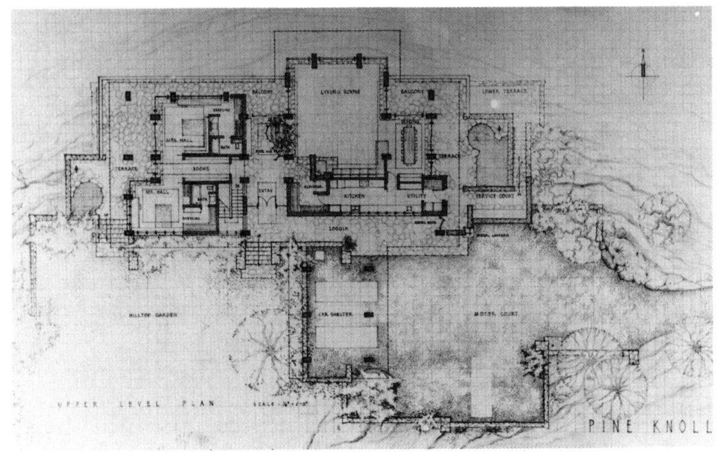

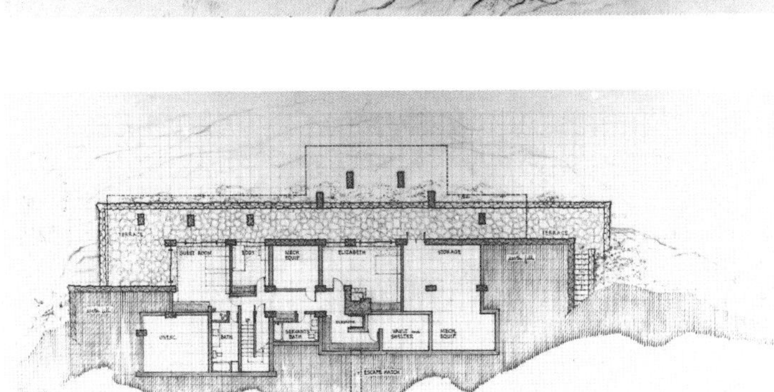

Opposite: Northwest view from the garden overlooking the Arkansas River.

Left: Columns anchor an interlocking plan of the upper level (above). The lower level includes a riverside arcade.

Entrance gate with lantern. The vertical gate, which swings down, is finely balanced.

Nine-foot overhangs dominate the south side of the house. Standing at the front door, stone retaining walls split apart for garden steps. A curving green arc of Chinese fir defines the hill-top garden.

Custom details continue into the main residence. A double-stemmed T, first manifested in steel on a lantern at the driveway entrance, reappears on stereo speaker grilles inside the house; ultimately the design motif ornaments sofa pillows needlepointed by the Halls' daughter-in-law.

Jones explains that the abstract geometry of the T design was not an arbitrary conceit, but evolved with the house design. "I had finished fifty sheets of construction drawings before I noticed certain design elements," he says. "They were not imposed." Instead, the late-emerging geometric theme served as a thread to weave throughout its fabric as the building coalesced.

Details fit into craftsmanlike interior space that flows with Wrightian ease out to gardens overlooking the river. Built-in sofas, bookcases, and shelves lend human scale to coffered and gabled living spaces. The current owners, Margaret and Chuck Ensminger, have continued the original owners' stewardship, making only minimal, careful alterations to interiors that still exude a sense of comfort and understated luxury.

Pine Knoll remains a milestone in Jones's career. The important commission with a prominent citizen increased his confidence as it took him beyond Fayetteville to the state's capital and largest city; subsequent publication in the national press widened the audience for his houses. Decades later, Pine Knoll continues to reflect Jones's affinity for his clients and his early skill at thoroughly integrated, craftsmanlike residential design. ▲

A lowered wood ceiling surrounds the vestibule pool. The hanging lantern and carpet date from the owners' diplomatic travels.

Above: The living room, looking north toward the river plain.

Right: Appalachian oak panels line the living room ceiling, washed in continuous light by cove fixtures. Chimney haunches catch the long beam.

Opposite: The dovecote built for the original owner's prized pigeons has since been converted into a playhouse.

117.

EDEN ISLE, ARKANSAS
1965

A remote location conceals the startling form of Stoneflower, Jones's most sensual house, reserving it for a private few. Tucked along a boulder-strewn hillside high above Greer's Ferry Lake in the resort community of Eden Isle, Arkansas, this small house, featured in *Life* in 1966, has been largely forgotten. Its importance to Jones's subsequent work and its potential influence on American architecture demand wider familiarity. Two of Jones's shelter prototypes—caves and treehouses—are fancifully synthesized in the house, which served as a working model for later, more complex projects.

Because skeletal programmatic demands centered on a rock-bottom budget, Jones employed minimal means to produce strong ideas. The architect had worked with the clients, two landscape architects employed in Eden Isle's initial design, who had traded their professional services for land in the new resort community. Curt Goodfellow had a young family; Bob Shaheen could help split expenses. They jointly contributed physical labor, lifting stones into place for site and foundation construction, which reduced the total cost to a manageable $25,000.

Inside and underneath the house, a rock foundation contributes a sense of physical drama. A womblike living space, its undulating rock walls warmed by skylights, surrounds and protects you. A bowed fireplace lights one corner of the man-made cave; a small fountain circulates water through a small interior pool. Rock ledges for seating, boulders for coffee tables, and a flagstone floor combine to form a Jungian dreamscape.

Unexpected mystery awaits exploration at ground level. A protected bathing grotto lies around a corner and down a lowered, darkened passage, where overhead sunlight illuminates ferns growing from the stone walls. With the turn of a spigot, a high waterfall drops from a stone ledge into a sunken pool. A stone lavatory and a toilet occupy an adjacent niche. No door separates the living area from the bathing area; placement and sight lines provide enclosure and privacy, an implied invitation to disrobe and play, as Eden Isle's name suggests.

If Stoneflower's undulating ground level represents an intuitive world, the main level's great, light-flooded end walls symbolize rationality. Jones combined living, sleeping, cooking, and eating in a single rectilinear space. Partial walls and an overhead loft separate functions, but no full walls break its high, narrow volume. Daytime visiting and nighttime sleeping take place in the

Opposite: Few houses in America approach Stoneflower's drama, set like a lighthouse beside a rocky outcropping above Greer's Ferry Lake.

View from the deck back toward the vacation residence.

huge space just off the exterior deck; the kitchen, tucked underneath the sleeping platform, divides dining from living.

Although a dichotomy between dark and light, male and female, cave and treehouse slices the building into two levels, a single energy unites the whole. Jones designed the building as a breathing, mechanical marvel. Air enters the consistently cool lower level and by convection rises to the roof, where it is expelled through movable eave-mounted windows. Interior screen doors allow glass walls to be opened at each end for additional circulation.

A wood deck, its thirty-foot extension equal to the building's interior length, extends Stoneflower's living area into the tree canopy. Flanking twin flambeaux (open metal vessels designed for grilling steaks and lighting the summer night) connect the cantilevered upper deck with its underbelly, where structural bracing nails deck to ground in a volumetric starburst of welded steel.

Stoneflower preceded and anticipated Jones's masterwork, Thorncrown Chapel. To stabilize the high walls of the house, the architect experimented with paired wood columns and overhead cross-bracing that he would again employ in the chapel. Outside, the house resembles Thorncrown in the massive wood diagonals of the glass end walls and the overhanging gable roof. But where Thorncrown is sheathed in glass, Stoneflower is sheathed in board-and-batten siding. In their proportions the buildings are akin. Stoneflower is exactly one-half the size of Thorncrown—12 feet wide, 30 feet long, and 24 feet high, versus the latter's 24 by 60 feet.

Although the house is small, it has a remarkable presence, which is derived in part from the surprise of its vertical walls lifted high above the lichen-covered boulders, in part from the marriage of opposed worlds united in one structure. Part hillside outcropping, part lighthouse, Stoneflower bristles with ideas and controlled energy. ▲

The building appears mated to mossy boulders. Vertical wood strips screen the rear elevation from errant golf balls off the nearby course.

Vertical ribs emphasize the twenty-four-foot height of the main level. Rope pulleys operate the windows at eave line to evacuate heat from the interior and encourage convective air movement. Angular skylights at the base of the wall (above and opposite) light the building's basement.

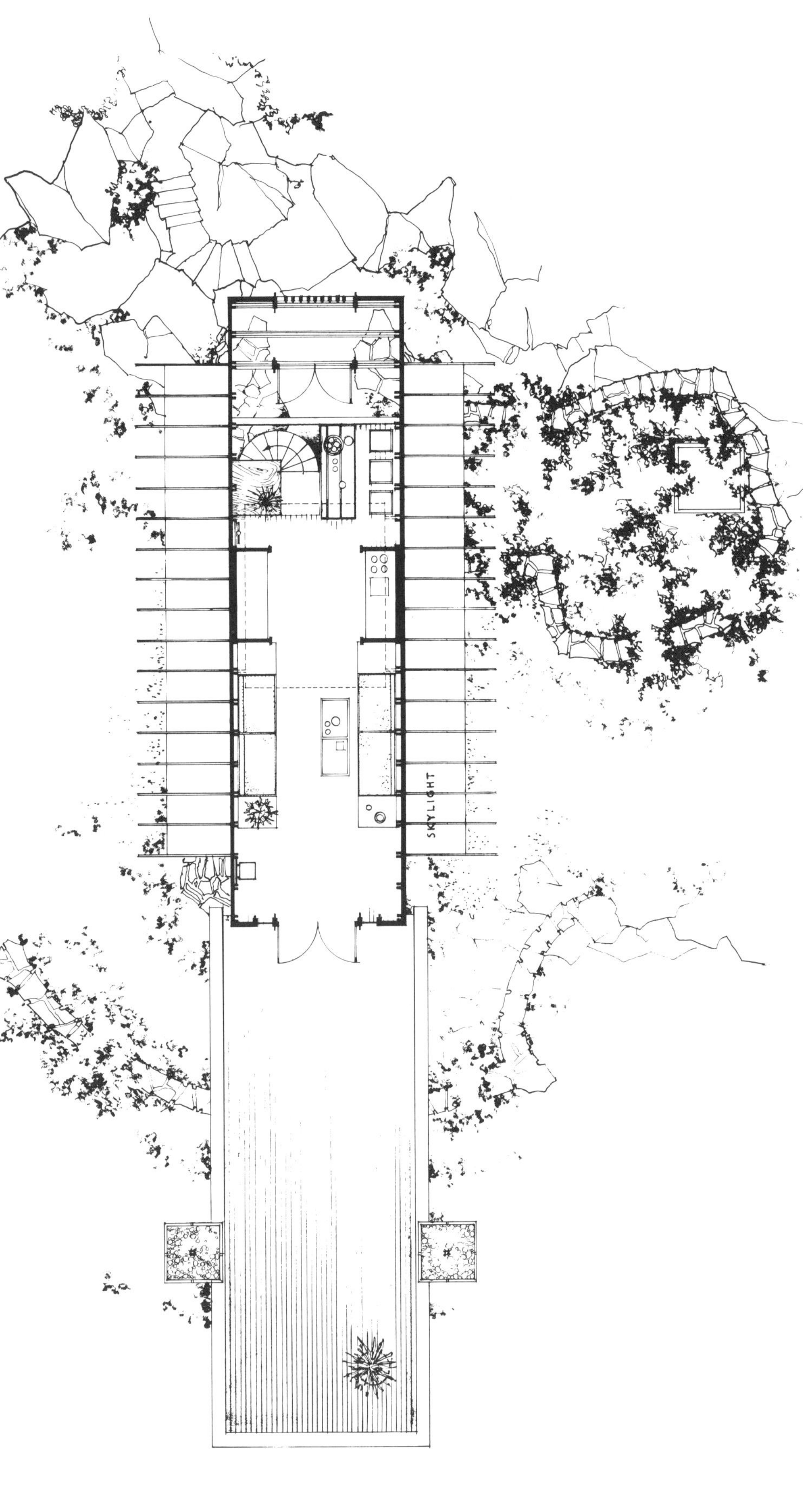

The upper-level plan is a variation on the "shotgun" type—a single, linear space. The interior space and deck are equally sized.

Right: View through to sleeping loft and Pullman-type kitchen.

A ribbon of continuous flooring from
the living space through to the deck;
lamps between wooden posts shine above
built-in sofa beds.

Unstable high walls demanded structural support. The resulting cross-bracing would appear in later work such as Thorncrown Chapel.

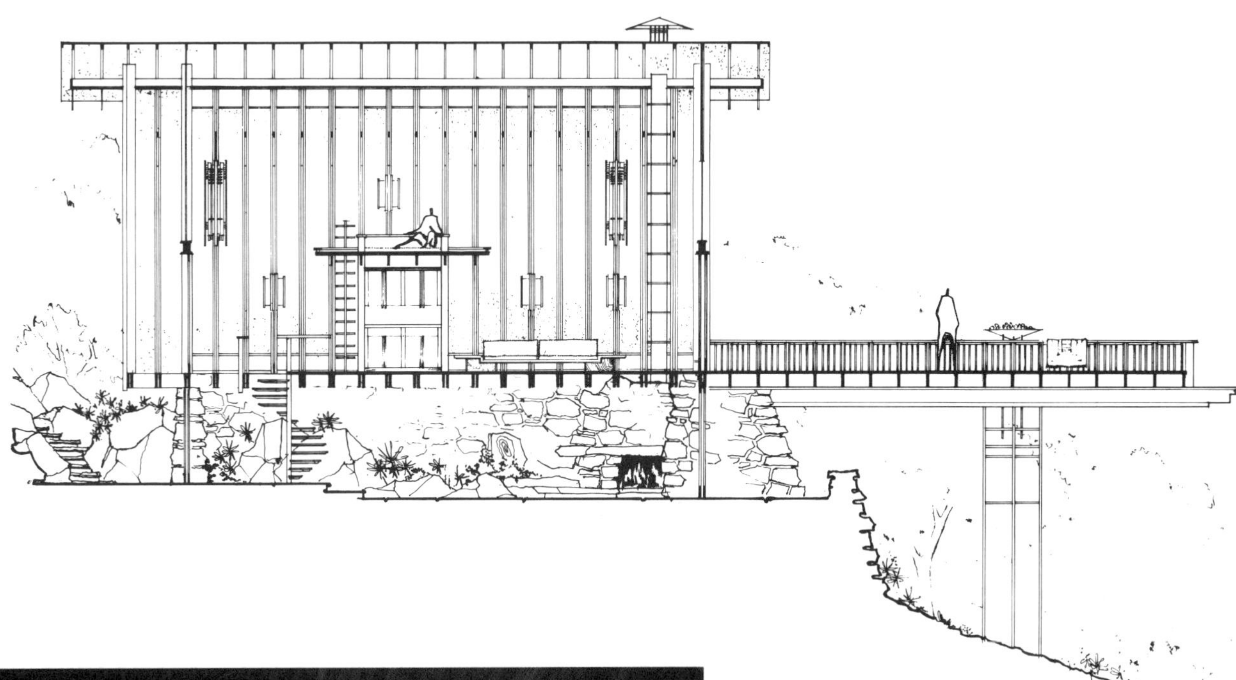

The section reveals a building separated from the natural bluff on an independent stone base.

View from dining area, looking through rear screen wall. The dining table rolls for multiple usage, while other furnishings and details are pared to a minimum.

The lower level plan shows the influence of Bruce Goff as it blurs the distinction between natural and man-made. Stones have been positioned to serve many functions: ledge, seating, and table.

An Edenic space. In the skylit bathing grotto, only sight lines separate the shower from the garden room.

Clear streams run beneath the Ozark bluffs. For an early private house outside Fayetteville, Jones placed the structure beside and over a partially dammed creek to create an idealized natural setting. "This house is an example of the operative opposite, of idealizing the site," says Jones. Its inspiration came not from Fallingwater, Wright's masterpiece beside a waterfall, Jones maintains, but from the French chateau Chenonceaux, which bridges the river Cher. Unlike formal Chenonceaux, which steps into the river, foundations for this craftsmanlike chateau run alongside the creek bank, then turn to both bridge and dam the flowing water.

Like Fallingwater, the house engages running water, but with obvious differences. "It is in opposition to Fallingwater," says Jones, "although I was after the same thing—interaction and interchange. There is an intangible caught in the middle . . . an important element." Fallingwater stands apart from the wild landscape, but this residence blends in. While Wright's house cantilevers from a bluff above a waterfall, Jones's house nestles in above its foundation.

Set in a private green valley at the foot of a bluff covered with dogwood and redbud trees, this residence seems far removed from the world, although it is located less than a block from the street. Siting makes the couple who live there feel in touch with nature. As one of them says: "You are constantly aware of what's going on [in the changing seasons]. In the winter there is the snow; in the spring, the birds."

The presence of water soaks the senses. When full of spring rain, the pond roars over its stone dam in a green sheet, creating a hum through the valley. During summer drought, water trickles through a key cut in the dam's flank. The entire west elevation of the house yields to the water view, with doors and windows opening to a continuous stone patio lining the pond. Stone walls drop to the water to form platforms for eating, sitting, or tethering canoes.

The architect, who, in his words, sought "not to recognize the windows and doors," found one answer in "transitional areas that flow to outdoor spaces and the garden." An optical illusion begins the merger where glass-walled latticework separates an indoor greenhouse from the exterior entryway. Projecting angular rafters overhead, their shake roofing stripped away and filled with glass, set a rhythm repeated along the opposite, waterside elevation. It is virtually impossible to discriminate enclosure from openness.

While the size of the interior is not grand, its effect is warmed by woods and its apparent space is multiplied by sleight of

NORTHWEST ARKANSAS
1960 AND 1972

The residence aligns itself with the still waters of a dammed pond in rural Arkansas, then turns to span the running stream beneath its spillway. A mounting bluff opposite the house borders an idealized garden.

Above: The strong horizontal lines of the roof, deck, and dam bring peace to an Arkansas valley. Unlike Fallingwater, Jones's waterside residence bridges its creek.

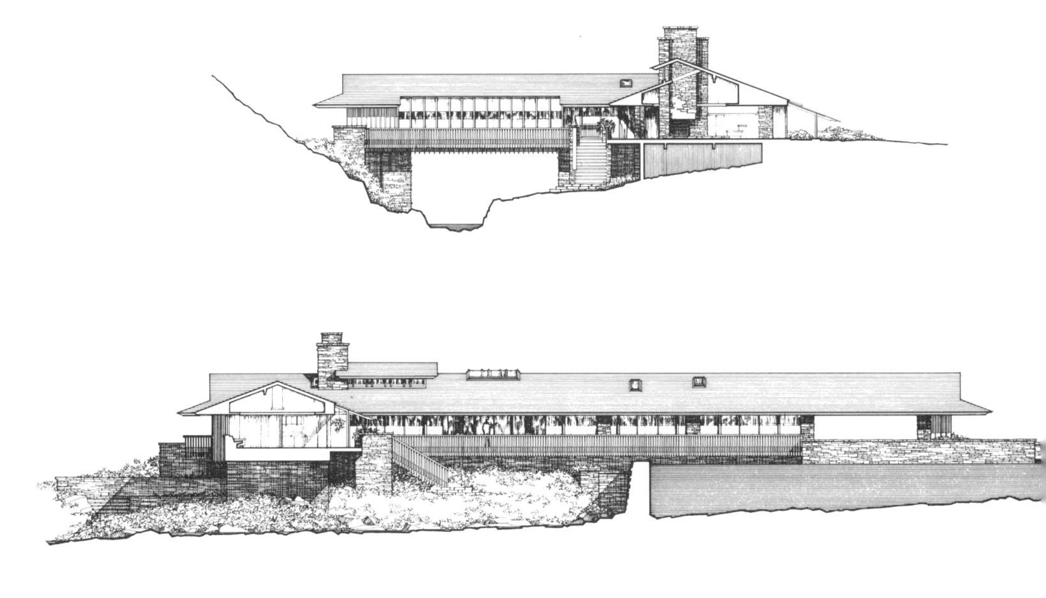

Shadows enliven roof joists, which extend beyond the garden room bridge.

hand. A skylight brings an expansive quality to the entry. Wooden screening on low ceilings contributes a perception of depth and height.

As Jones puts it, building materials "help to string out the transitional areas," heightening the "indoor-outdoor relationship. Wood is as good a material inside as outside. The same [stone] floor is used indoors as well as outdoors." Similarly, the exterior siding is repeated inside in wood battens and trim, which highlight the creamy ceilings. Welcoming comfort distinguishes the living spaces.

Parts of the house are forceful. Stone columns, fieldstone floors (except for strip oak flooring in the living room to complement the owners' Turkish rugs), and wood (in custom furnishings, lanterns and lighting, ceilings, and exterior window framing) create a strong base, physically and psychologically.

A strong base was important when Jones's first house for the owners, constructed in 1960, had to be rebuilt. "We had four kids when our house burned in 1972," says the owner. "By the time we built the second house, they had graduated from college and were out in the world." The owners were committed to their valley site and moved into a mobile home on the property during the two-year reconstruction interval.

While there is a similar "ground pattern" to the plan, Jones added a new master bedroom to the building's south end and inserted three guest rooms into what had been the master bedroom suite. The guest bedrooms' private porches now face north to woods and pastureland; the master bedroom faces the pond. An interior basement stair was moved to an outside wall to widen the living room.

As time has passed, the children's bunk beds have yielded to a garden room filled with grandchildren's toys and a desk. Operable windows allow the cool air that follows the creek to flow through the long room overlooking the waterfall.

Although this house does not exhibit the formal rigor of Jones's later work, it tempers pragmatism with sensitivity to nature and a strong sense of shelter. Permeating the atmosphere, yet not overwhelming it, are the creek and bluff of the idealized natural garden it inhabits. ◬

The floor plan, as altered after a fire in 1972.

Below: The long house sits within a thirty-acre compound near the heart of a small Arkansas community. A long shake roof and western red cedar walls screen the creek.

The outdoor arbor continues through to a glassed conservatory at the entrance, creating the illusion of continuing outdoor space.

View from the dining room to the vestibule and living area. The lantern, table, dining chairs, and bench were all designed by Jones.

Above, top: A moon-formed masonry wall in silhouette against the conservatory's eastern daylight.

Looking north in the gabled living space, the western wall opens to the deck, and built-in wood cabinetry lines a recessed east wall. The concrete lintel in the stone chimney was etched by Jones to emphasize its crafted aspect. Photo above (right) shows modifications after fire. Shelving and cabinet work replace built-in sofa and interior stair, seen at left.

Raheen, the Robert Alexander residence, dramatically mediates between man and nature. Set on the edge of a rock bluff several hundred feet above the Hazel Valley, the building hovers over emerald pastureland. Choosing the spectacular site from among the Alexanders' 600 acres was the project's critical decision.

An implicit trust between client and architect spanned the Atlantic Ocean. After a brief initial meeting in Fayetteville, the owners, a corporate executive and his wife, left for a year's business sojourn in England. In the meantime, they asked Jones to help choose a spot for the house and to begin its design. "Basically, we left him alone," says Mrs. Alexander.

After rejecting the site of an existing farmhouse beside the White River, Jones walked the property with his wife to select a stone bluff. The absentee clients agreed and gave Jones oversight of most details, since they could only return to Arkansas for brief, semi-annual visits during the three-year construction period. The view from the chosen site, which stretches across the river valley to a parallel ridge, encompasses most of the property and stretches into a smoky distance.

Today a road angles across the Alexanders' lower pastures, cuts past ascending boulders beside a rill, and grinds in a final push to the open summit. Cars park on a hilltop made bald by grazing cattle; trees line the perimeter. Ahead, the openness of the cliffside flank is blocked by bits of roofs, chimneys, low walls, and courtyards that combine to create the welcoming impression of a small village on a hilltop.

A garden gate invites visitors into a sheltered garden courtyard of Japanese maples and man-made sculpture. Scaly roofs and stone walls screen outside views. The entrance, protected beneath a skylit overhanging roof, is to the left; the turn reorients the visitor, providing a psychological effect similar to the Oriental custom of removing one's shoes upon entering a house.

The plan for this large house is F-shaped. The longest part of the house faces the valley and contains living, dining, and entertaining spaces, and a "cattery" (quarters for the owners' prize-winning felines). One of the two shorter wings contains bedrooms; the other houses the owners' antique cars. The twin wings intimate security and stability on the exposed hilltop, apparently anchoring the building to solid ground.

The interior is multileveled, in response to the site's slope toward the bluff. From the vestibule, one steps down to dining space,

OUTSIDE FAYETTEVILLE
ARKANSAS
1975

Multiple wings, walls, and roofs set above the Hazel Valley, in a residential blend resembling a hilltop village.

then down again to the living area, which opens out to the pool and to the sky. The view through the house shoots from the front door through the living room to a long deck, cantilevered like a celestial diving platform.

The sunny living room perches on the bluff's edge, open through a southwest-facing corner window. Stone columns and stepped platforms interrupt and anchor the horizontal flow. A broad fieldstone chimney with a gigantic stone lintel grounds the aerie, as do substantial structural roof beams, reinforced by a bridgework of paired wooden struts.

The primary circulation path parallels the bluff's edge and remains at a constant grade; access to the twin wings extends from the main spine. One of the house's grandest spaces, the bedroom corridor, connects the bedroom wing to the body of the house in a rhythmic spatial procession marked by wood storage units, wood battens along the ceiling, and thirteen windows along the corridor wall. All the bedrooms, including the master suite, open off this long corridor and face the pool and southern sun. Each room has wide southern glazing covered by a deeply overhanging roof.

Outside the bedrooms, the sound of water fills the cliff-side courtyard. Mr. Alexander explains that the decision to locate a waterfall at the end of the pool was "belatedly conceived," though at his request. Large sliding doors were removed from the bedroom wing to accommodate the seven-ton boulder, which was rolled into place and plumbed as a waterfall.

Water from the boulder cascades into an indigo pool. Stepped stone platforms narrow as they rise. As is true elsewhere, this exterior space is both open and contained, bordered on two sides by a continuous low roofline and the solidity of edges.

Permanence is implied in the design of Raheen, whose Gaelic name translates as "fortress." Raheen's bones—stone platforms, walls, and pillars broadly and boldly placed on a high cliff—seem, like Taliesin West, native American. Perhaps Jones's most dramatically sited residence, Raheen ceremoniously merges earth and air. ◬

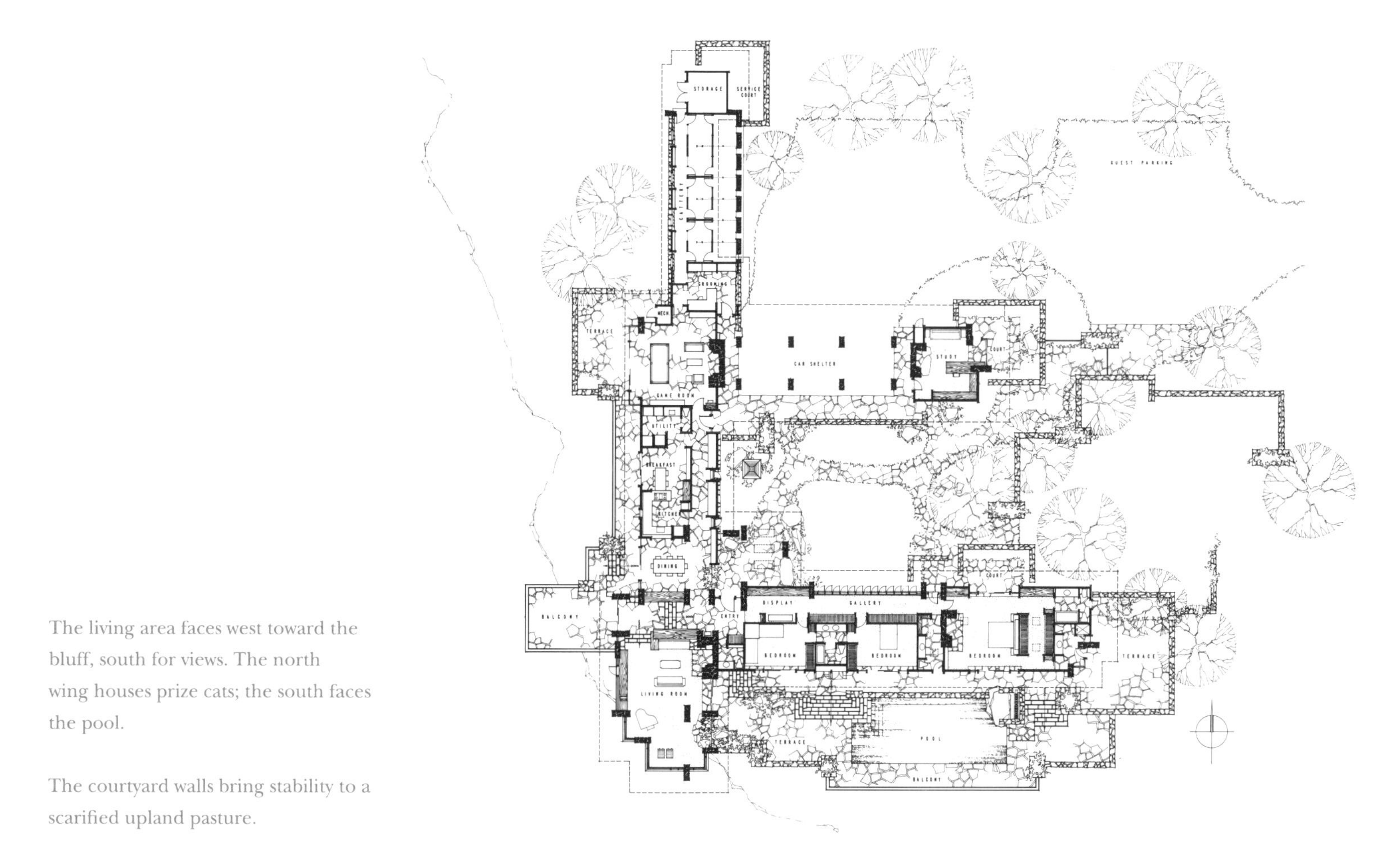

The living area faces west toward the bluff, south for views. The north wing houses prize cats; the south faces the pool.

The courtyard walls bring stability to a scarified upland pasture.

Columns and an overhanging roof shield a transparent living space at the southwest corner. A clerestory window fills the void beneath the upper gable.

A multilevel interior drops from the dining area, with its custom furnishings, to the living area.

The merger of indoors and out. Jones dissolves the southwest edge through a large glazed opening, a butt-jointed glass corner. An emphatic stone structure and sheltering roof underscore a sense of permanence.

This house relates to its private lake like a boat making way. Water dominates the small estate, located twelve miles west of Little Rock on thirty acres of private woodland. With four towers and three large triangular roofs cantilevered into the wind, the house presents a strong, active image in a dreamy landscape.

With reason. The idea for the design came to Jones quickly as he lay recuperating from open-heart surgery. "I woke up with the image of the house," he says. "It was not from having thought about how many bedrooms or baths: that is not the way I usually work. I tested the idea by the house's requirements, and it all worked out. Usually in my work, a form 'becomes' from the plan or section; here, I was faced with a 'form-image.'"

Ideas had been boiling in Jones's imagination. He mentions historic design precedents: from France, the turreted chateau Azay-le-Rideau, set in a clearly defined pond beside the river Indre; from Japan, the Golden Pavilion. Louis Kahn's influence is visible in the four towers, each of which serves the building (as storage, bath, and air-conditioning equipment room) as it contributes to overall stability and form.

The soul of the allusive building is more American pie than Gallic, more lakeside park pavilion than floating temple. Designed as a year-round country residence for an active family, simplicity and uncluttered design characterize the construction materials. Rough-sawn siding covers both interior and exterior walls; solid concrete is common to the floors, fireplace, and exterior retaining walls; sliding glass panels surround the ground floor.

Axial symmetry characterizes the open plan. The two-story living space contains a central conversation area around a raised hearth, a central chimney, a divided grand stairway, and an encircling gallery walkway. A patio on the east side is balanced by another on the west side, and a west bedroom by an east bedroom. Pairing occurs in duplicate structural beams throughout the building.

Hierarchy controls placement in the symmetrical plan. The auxiliary living spaces (dining, recreation, and waterside seating), set apart by modulated ceiling heights and raised flooring, act as volumetric buffers to the out-of-doors. The kitchen and laundry are positioned in a spine extending back toward the hills.

Spectacular bedrooms hang over the water. Their ceilings run continuously from gable to floor, and large triangular windows fill each end. Free from intermediate support, they open to the lake. A tentlike master bedroom is positioned where the gable roof hits the

OUTSIDE LITTLE ROCK
ARKANSAS
1977

The four towers anchor the house to its dramatic lakeside site. The dock extends the outdoor living space past a concrete bulkhead toward the water.

building's central pavilion, creating a skylit attic hideaway from which the current owner watches the evening stars and thunderstorms that fill the Arkansas nights.

The owners rarely use air conditioning, instead relying on lake breezes, shade from overhanging roofs, and convection currents that take air into, up, and through the structure as through a chimney. The family spends the best days on the decks and patios, fishing, launching boats, and watching the raucous waterfowl.

The architect married usefulness to a visionary central idea to make a comfortable American lake house, wide open and welcoming to family and guests. Viewed from a distance, however, the house becomes an idealized form among the hills; like a Hiroshige print, it is Jones's contemporary interpretation of the floating world. ▲

A transparent bedroom hangs cantilevered above the dock.

A central hearth establishes axial symmetry in this cruciform plan. Extensive decks surround the main floor. The upper level contains four bedrooms.

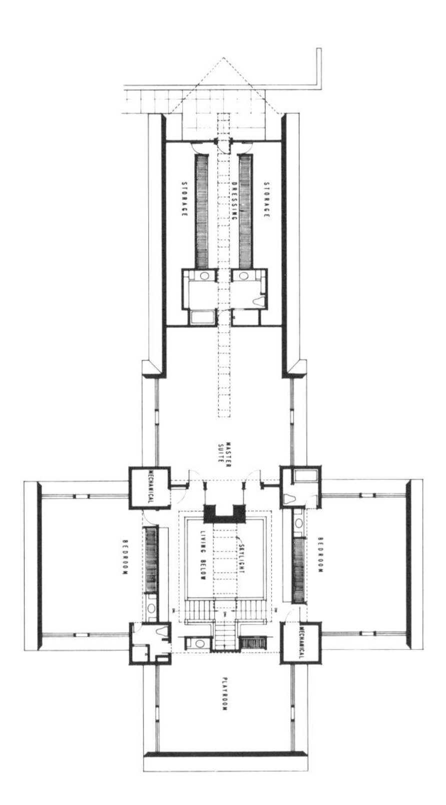

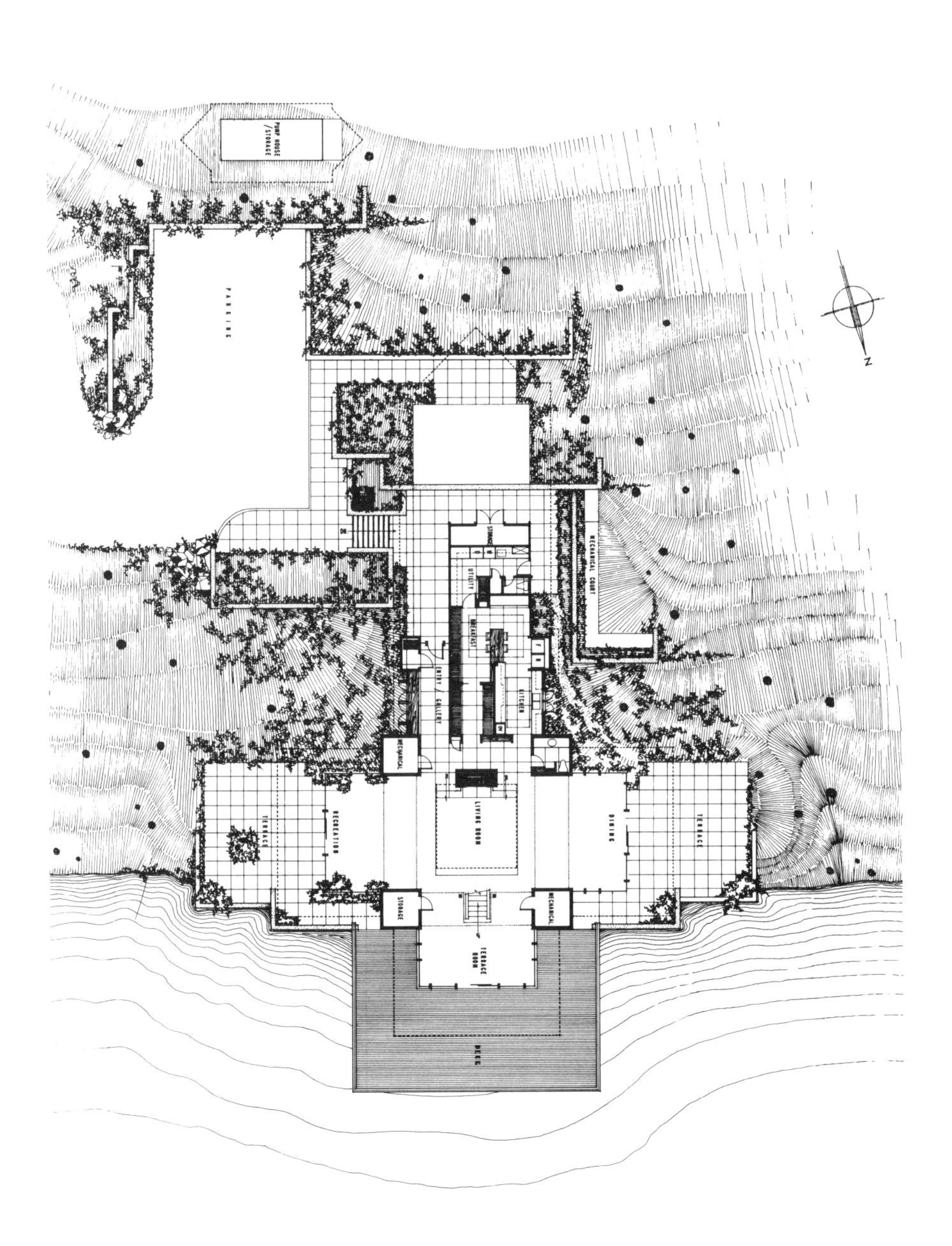

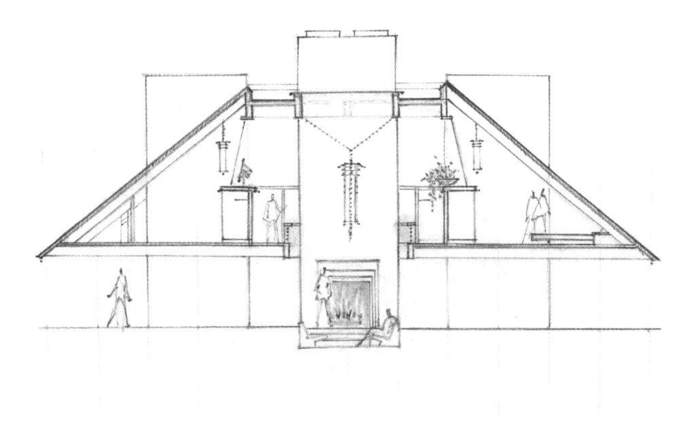

The service wing reaches landward under a long roof; the master bedroom stretches beneath a skylight.

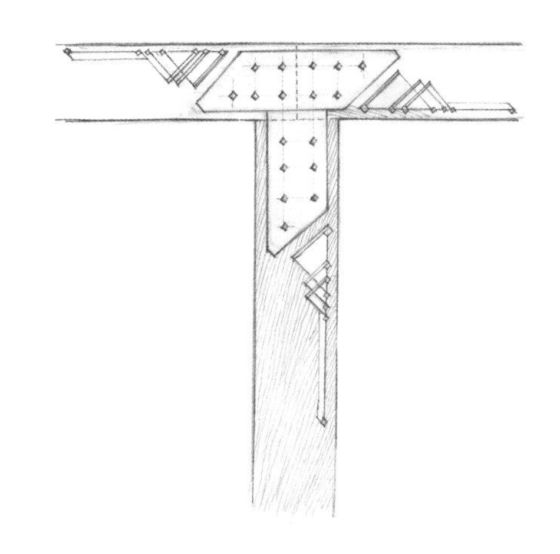

In the concrete chimney and rough-sawn wood walls, simple materials prevail inside and out.

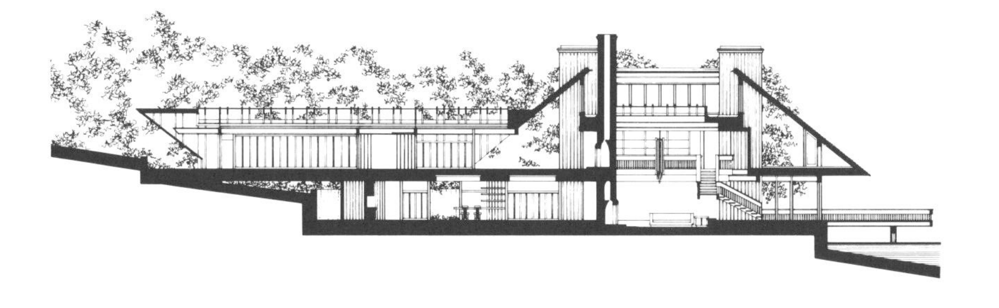

The section emphasizes the building's land-based form, open volumes, and relationship with water.

Opposite: View from second-floor balcony showing lantern and grand staircase.

Natural light is a dramatic element in all second-floor bedrooms.

The Lutz residence, a 2,600-square-foot, two-bedroom house, compresses a body of experience into one building as it presages new directions in Jones's architecture. It is a crossroads house, linked to Eden Isle's Stoneflower, built thirteen years earlier, and to Thorncrown Chapel, completed in 1980.

Like Stoneflower, the Lutz house advances into the treetops on an Ozark mountain slope; as at Stoneflower, water lies within view (Table Rock Lake, located on the border of Missouri and Arkansas). Both houses rest on masonry foundations; the Lutz house cantilevers above the solidity of a sixteen-foot-square pedestal.

Although Stoneflower was designed for weekend and vacation use and the Lutz house was intended as a year-round residence for a television writer and his wife, both harbor a single, powerful space. Only three privacy doors separate the Lutzs' open plan, which consists of a master bedroom loft opening to a living space, a study, and a second bedroom. A grand, interlocking stair unique among Jones's stock, entered at mid-level from an exterior bridge, connects sleeping and living areas.

One detail, the building's cross-bracing, figuratively links the design to Jones's past and present work. The high walls of the building's central open space, like those at Stoneflower, demanded rigidity for the structural frame, says Maurice Jennings. High crossed wooden Xs solved the problem at Shell Knob as they had at Eden Isle. Cross-bracing would appear with greater resonance at Thorncrown Chapel. What Jones calls a "discontinuous connector," the diamond-shaped metal ring joining the bracing members, first appears at the Lutz house.

Continuity in Jones's design throughout three decades is apparent in the Lutz residence: its spatial quality, central hearth, and openness suggest the later Reed residence at Hogeye. Parts of the residence seem ecclesiastical—the entry bridge, opaque board-and-batten walls, stepped gabled roof, and glazed end wall are comparable to those at Thorncrown Worship Center.

While it joins a continuum of earlier and later buildings, the Lutz house broadens our understanding of the nature of Jones's originality. What began as a revision of earlier ideas receives, from Jones's hand, a clear identity; what might have been old becomes something new.

SHELL KNOB, MISSOURI
1978

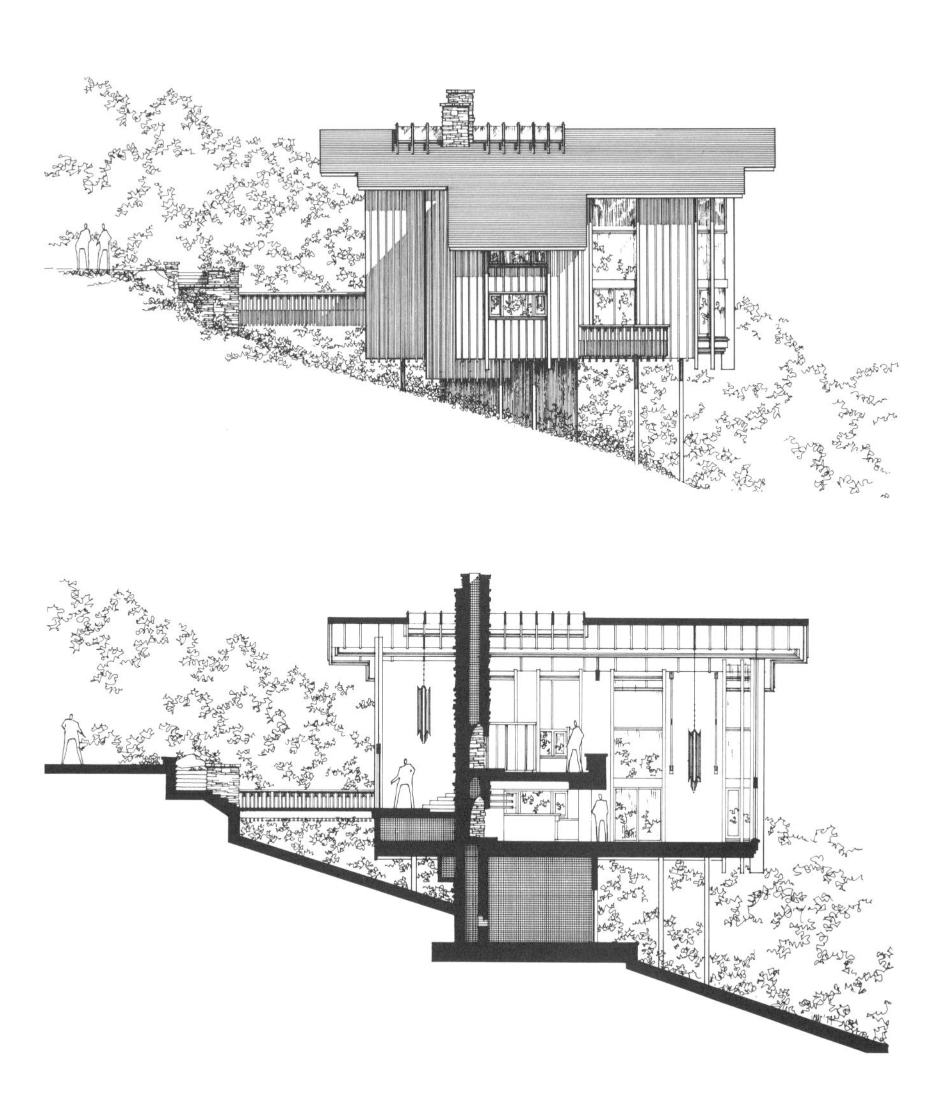

Stone walls, pathway, and bridge to the front door presage the entrance to Thorncrown Worship Center.

A steep grade is evident in both the elevation and section. The structure rests on a sixteen-foot-square masonry plinth. Note the high living space below the intermediate entry, and the higher sleeping platform.

Metal wall brackets tie cross-bracing to internal structure, and metal rings, which predate those at Thorncrown Chapel, link wooden bracing.

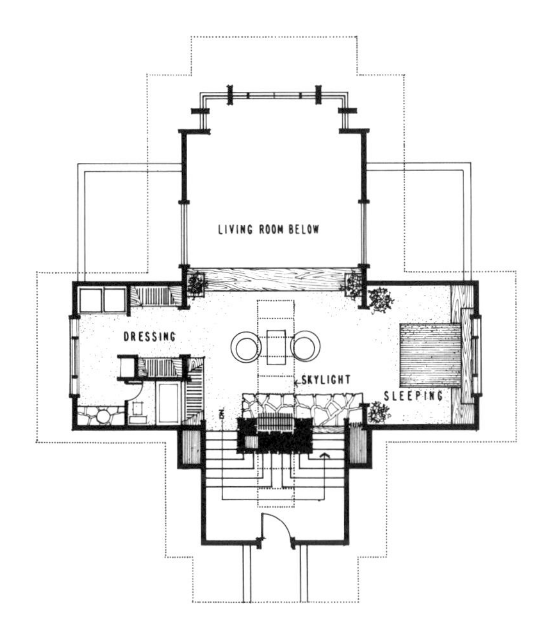

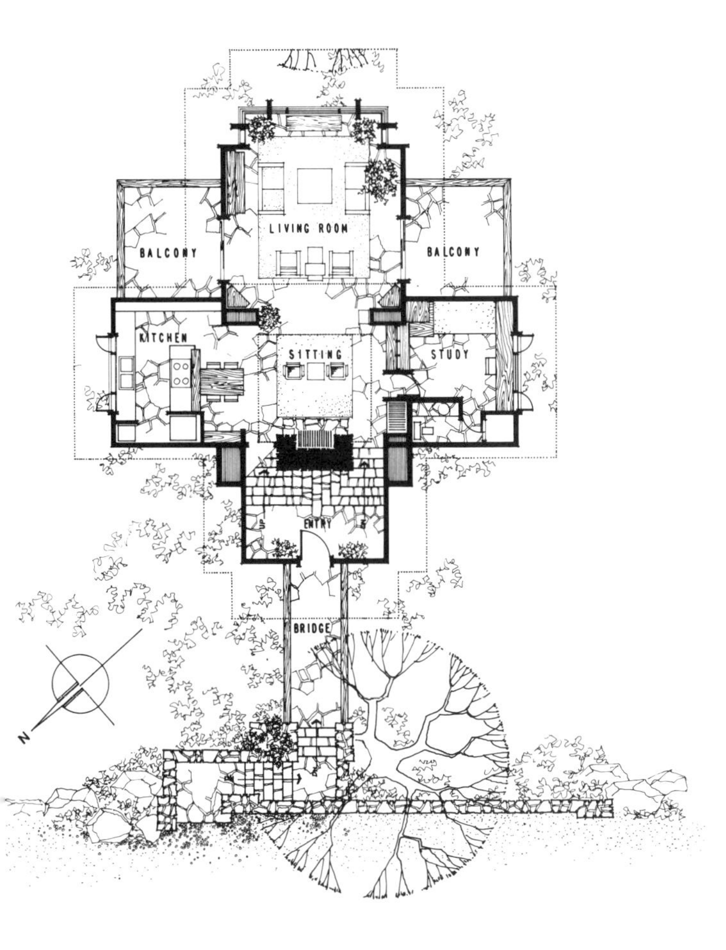

The cruciform plan suggests later chapel work.

He is the dangdest fellow I ever saw in my life. He's seeing things you or I don't even notice. Like a shadow on a wall from a tree.

JIM FINCH, CONTRACTOR

Leaves all but obscure the Edmondson residence, set on a three-acre ravine near the Arkansas delta

Opposite: The guesthouse and trellis rest within a tree canopy

FORREST CITY
ARKANSAS
1983

Footsteps, not vision, measure the true size of the Edmondson house: a blizzard of leaves that surrounds both residence and outbuildings obscures all but glimpses of the total design. To grasp the property's length and breadth, one rambles down an orchestrated pathway through tree-shrouded buildings and grounds. Essayist Henry Plummer caught the project's spirit in his book, *The Potential House*, when he described it as "spilling downhill . . . a kind of miniature forest . . . offering dimensions of voyage."

The Edmondson house may be Jones's most thorough residential ensemble. Clients Don and Ellen Edmondson commissioned the architect to design not only buildings and walkways but also small things such as dishware. Even a baby's crib bears Jones's geometric flourish. Although the hundreds of small details are experienced individually, the mind connects the disparate pieces into wholeness.

Edmondson was anxious to build what he called an "energy-efficient, light-filled tree house" on a plunging ravine across from an earlier small house. Through marriage, he inherited two daughters; later in life, after both daughters were grown and had moved, he and his wife acquired an additional child. With each family variation, the Edmondsons' needs changed, and the house, which steps down the hill in a series of buildings and terraces, reflects the dynamics of their family life.

Just off the suburban street, behind a low stucco wall, a car shelter occupies the site's highest ground. Brick steps lead downward in a descending sequence that drops with the land to cross a bridge, passes through the tall main residence, and drops past a pool house to a pagoda/boathouse. A sixteen-acre lake completes the path.

Jones united the composition with creamy stucco walls, red tile roofs, red pavers on walks and patios, and pools. Tile and stucco, unusual choices for the architect, were requested by the Edmondsons for the four-level, 6,000-square-foot main structure, which stands straight up among the surrounding tulip poplars.

The floor plan, with four heated living areas in two major buildings, provides the clients the luxury of choice. Friends gather on summer evenings under the high-ceilinged main living space; a screened porch overlooking the pool invites reading or quiet visiting. The main residence contains two sleeping areas—ground-level bedrooms opening onto a private sitting room and a third-level master suite. The guesthouse offers a private hearth and its own greenhouse.

Jones regulated interior spaces for variety and for psychological effect, from a low ceiling in the intimate library, where

golden coals warm an open hearth, to double height in the summer living room. All the rooms have treetop views.

Interior walls, like the facades, are stucco. The millwork is red oak, sanded and sealed, with a darker redwood highlighting major beams. Dark or light, "there is not a piece of wood that hasn't been milled or worked," says the building contractor, Jim Finch, who directed four workers. The plans exceeded 100 pages, although "there never was a complete set. They kept adding to them," says Finch.

The steep site presented specific construction challenges for the builder. The buildings rise among foliage with the stoutness of tree trunks, a feat that involved cutting only one tree, "a dying oak," according to Edmondson. Jones's conservation ethic heightened the project's naturalistic effect but made the entire construction process "tough," says Finch, because, as with construction of Thorncrown Chapel, building materials had to be "toted in, one piece at a time."

Finch's crew constructed most of the pieces on-site, including finished carpentry. Carpenters even cut and assembled the house's elaborate wooden lanterns (which Finch likens to Tinker Toys) under the car shelter roof. The front door took two men a month to build. Most challenging, perhaps, was the patio trellis. "There is over one mile of linear footage of redwood in the trellis alone. And it is all pegged," Finch says.

The union of trellis, house, and houseware into a cohesive composition echoes Wright's goal of fully integrated composition. Yet the Edmondson property demonstrates Jones's emergence from Wright's shadow: quiet assurance characterizes the planning and spatial composition; humility characterizes the subordination of building image to the site's fullness. No sculpture or fountain, walkway or room overshadows the naturalistic unity in this evolving house, a touchstone of Jones's maturity.

Opposite: A range of materials at the entrance to the four-story house includes stucco walls, a tile roof, and brick pavers, uncharacteristic building materials for the architect.

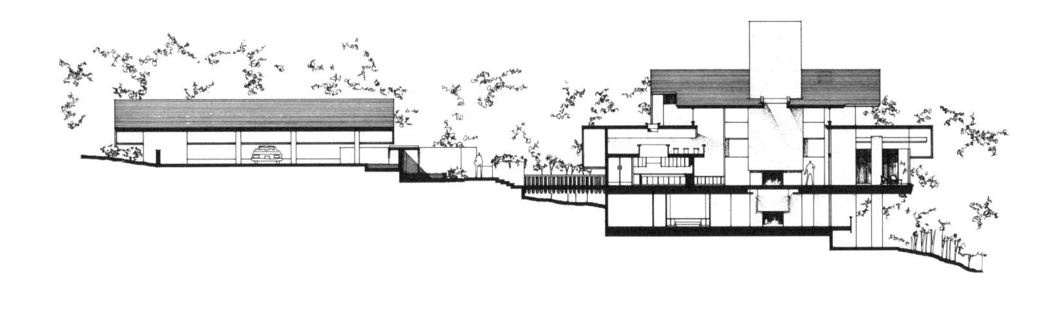

A descending pathway begins at the car shelter, drops to a plaza, and crosses a bridge to the main living level. This early section does not show the guesthouse, which was added later.

Thick stucco walls block the suburban street. Jones compares his metal sculpture, fabricated of sawed and bent steel, to a "linear accelerator."

The mass of the hearth separates the two main living spaces of the first floor.

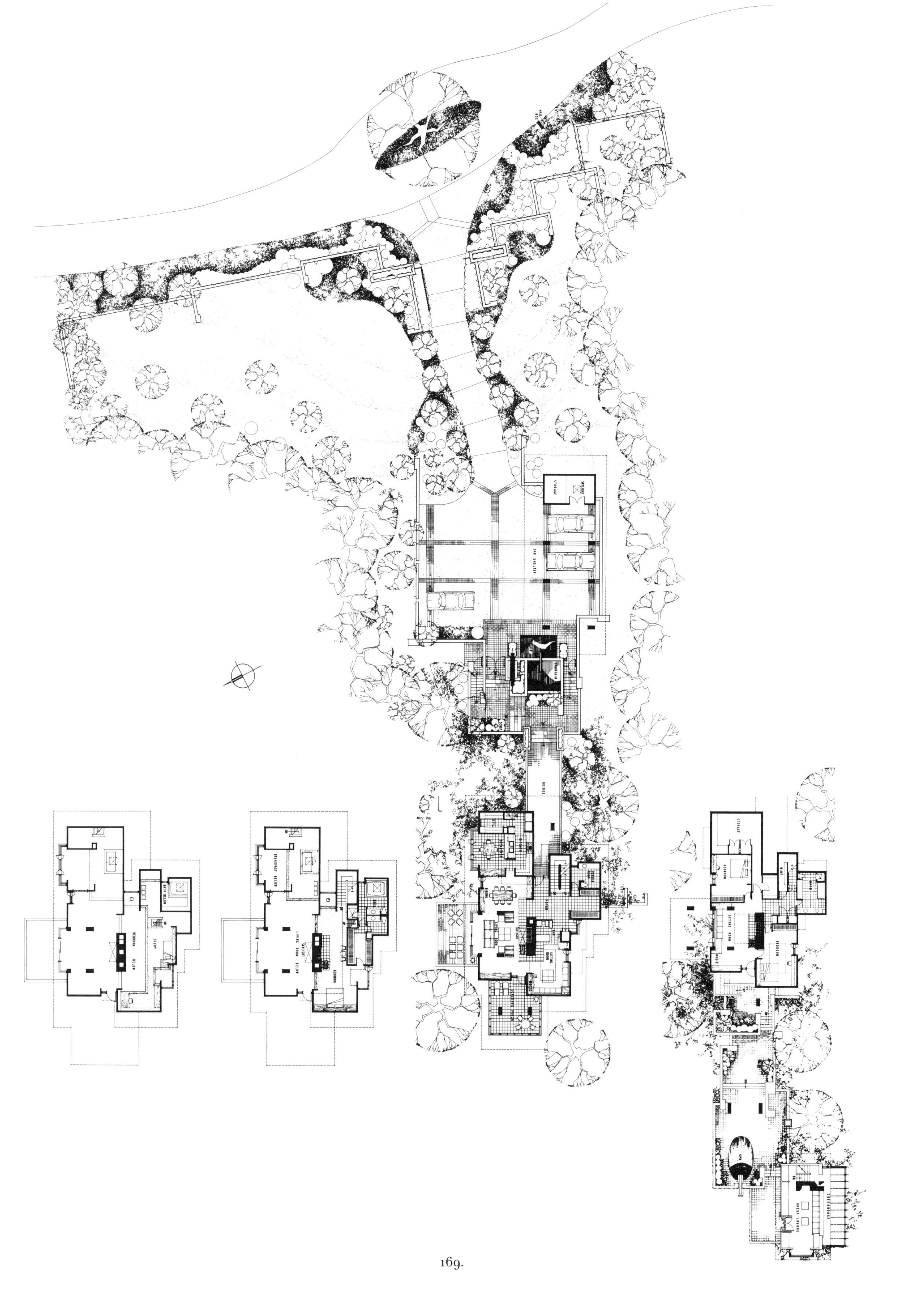

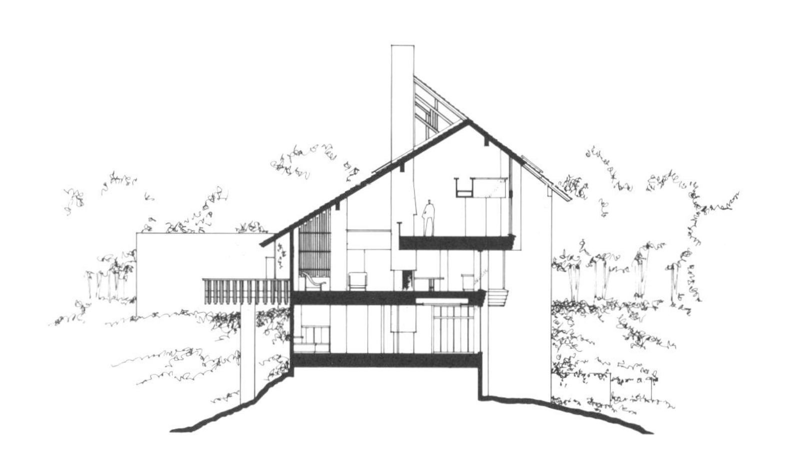

Above: Narrow windows in the dining room frame the owners' signature "E."

Views of the master bedroom, from the private sitting area and from the balcony study. The bedroom opens to the living room below, evident in the section at right.

HOGEYE, ARKANSAS
1983

I would not be at all distressed if I could only use a simple gable roof, post and beam, and a simple rectangle for the rest of my life.

FAY JONES

Roy and Norma Reed's farm offers refuge from the open countryside. Located some ten miles outside Fayetteville near tiny Hogeye, Arkansas, the Reeds' sloping acreage holds one of Fay Jones's pivotal works, a residence that combines great simplicity and ingenuity. While this unpretentious house is filled with contemporary ideas, it was inspired by the classic American barn and belongs to the farm. A foundation wall of native stone and wood siding closely ties the building to the forty-acre hillside setting of woodland and rolling pasture.

When Reed, a former *New York Times* correspondent, returned to teach and to write in his native Arkansas, he and his wife sought an unfussy, economical residence to shield their quiet pursuits. Minimal energy consumption was an important requirement. Their programmatic constraints provided a framework for creative thought: the rustic structure they built is more elegant and more important than its nominal 2,300 square feet. Its simplicity and clarity distinguish it as among Jones's most accessible residential designs.

Clarity should not be mistaken for a lack of sophistication, however. The house at Hogeye turns a different face to each point of the compass. From the west, it is shielded from the sun by deciduous trees, a low roofline, and a porch above a native fieldstone base. From the east, the ascending roof, surmounted by a wooden ladder, almost kisses the ground. Large windows, including a rotated square on the south elevation, fill the building's strong gable ends.

Like most barns, the Reeds' residence is clad in wood. Silvery shakes cover the roof; walls of diagonally applied red cedar siding provide a natural texture. Jones says he intended the diagonal siding to relate the building to the old corn cribs prevalent in the area, yet the Reed residence also evokes other wood building traditions, particularly those of Japan and northern Europe.

Like the post-and-beam construction of traditional Japanese building, the structural system at Hogeye can be seen from outside. Like screens in early Japanese houses, sliding walls open the Reed residence to the prevailing breezes that rise from the valley; like Japanese houses, the interior is essentially one large volume.

Kinship with Oriental traditions does not relegate the house at Hogeye to the impractical or esoteric. The large windows (like "hayloft windows," says Jones) can be opened for air to rise through the high volume and out the gable ends. In fact, energy consciousness, "deeply embedded in the architecture" according to Jones, informs the building's organization. The second floor of the house overhangs

The western facade of the Reed home, looking uphill. A wide roof shades the porch and basement wall below.

the first to shade the south elevation; a broad roof shields the east elevation; a comfortable, undercut porch protects the west wall. At the basement level, a fieldstone wall collects solar heat on sun-filled days. In summer the stone, shaded by trees, provides mass to insulate the lower level.

As a measure of owner's and architect's conviction, the house lacks both central heat and air conditioning, relying upon convection and natural breezes to cool the interior and sunlight and a central hearth to keep the house warm. With two wood stoves and heavy insulation, sometimes "it gets too hot," says Reed, necessitating the opening of windows. The stove's twin flues, simple terra-cotta tiles clamped together by metal braces along thin metal columns, radiate heat and enliven the sixteen-foot-tall central living area.

The flue tiles and their supporting columns pinpoint the house's soaring single volume, a space that rises from strip oak flooring to the underside of the gabled roof. Mediating the height is a loft containing two bedrooms, baths, and a catwalk that circles a light-flooded living space. The finishes—painted walls and stained wood trim—are spare and simple.

An Oriental sensibility and American pragmatism imbue the small Reed residence with simplicity and economy. Its uncommon dignity, common sense, and strong originality, however, surpass both the sources of its inspiration and its apparent size.

The building's shed form resembles the American barn. A north window opens for ventilation; a ladder reaches a skylight for summer screening.

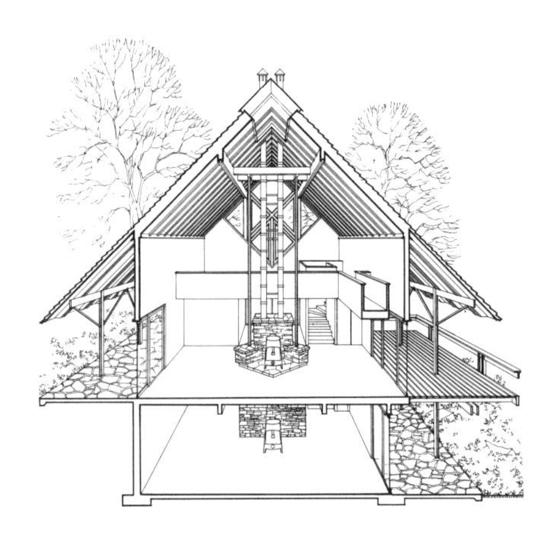

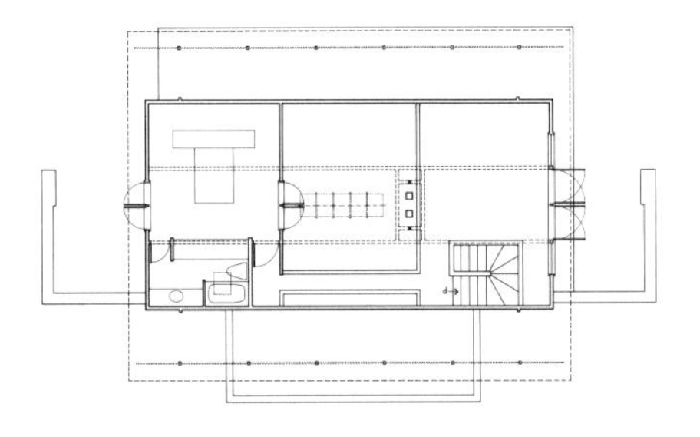

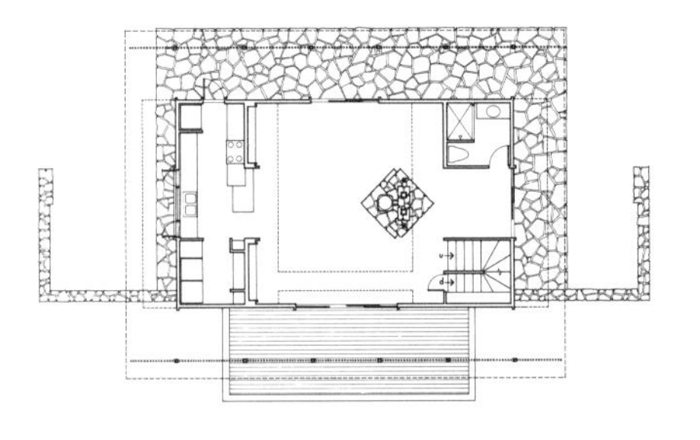

The upper level of the interior, facing north toward the catwalk. The ample volume of the main living space, accented by spare detailing and sculptural terra-cotta flues from the metal stove.

Steeply pitched roofs shed heavy snows at the Davenport house, placed on five acres of Rocky Mountain terrain.

Evergreen, Colorado, is "Rocky Mountain High" country, where ragged stone outcroppings and dark green conifers confront the sky. Here, mountain soil and fresh climate call for more vigorous buildings than the soft, ancient Ozarks. Unless met with bold design, the looming Rockies can overwhelm human structures.

Clustered angles, driven like stakes into the mineral-rich soil, tie down the Davenport residence. Jones created a compact, angular building in response to heavy snow loads and strong winds present at the site's 7,400-foot elevation. Towers, reminiscent of Jones's 1977 lakeside house near Little Rock, and a prowlike gabled roof oppose the elements. The building looks as if it could whistle but remain anchored in a high wind.

The client's program was simple: two bedrooms and two well-lit artist's studios. Like the Reed house at Hogeye, this house is centered, with all subservient spaces open to a central, grand living room. Both residences share unfussy detailing and both carry big ideas.

But unlike the Reeds' simple house, skewed orthogonal geometry orders both plan and section of the Davenport residence. The pieces of the plan in Evergreen—bedrooms, bathrooms, kitchen—are interlocked in a complex pattern. Rooms are clustered in diamond-shaped bundles on either side of the main living space; two triangular towers contain chimney and mechanical stacks.

The structural simplicity is beguiling. Exposed, scissored rafters carry the angular theme to the articulated framing system, and clean walls showcase exposed wood members.

Contrasting materials heighten the interior drama. Stone floors abut blonde strip-oak flooring near the hearth; oak chimney-side seating separates stone floor from wood, its yellow warmth highlighted by blue cushions. A central cast-concrete fireplace rises from wide hearth to slender chimney, the latter set apart like a ribbon from battened wood side walls.

And everywhere, light. Since the artist-client wanted and received a profusion of illumination, Jones let sunlight enter triangular clerestory windows formed by the juncture of the exterior towers and the roof. Windows in the end walls expose the interior to the eastern hillside and to the long view west.

EVERGREEN, COLORADO
1984

The prowlike roof and stone terrace of the west elevation. A ribbed balcony opens off the studio.

The Colorado site's longer views, taller mountains, and stony soil differ dramatically from Jones's typical Ozark sites. And, although the Davenport residence's towers, focused center, and simplicity recall the Arkansas houses, this mountain house belongs to Evergreen. If Jones's work is regional, the Davenport house clearly states that regionalism, at its best, is not imposed but is responsive to place. ▲

The client, an architectural delineator, required well-lit, dual studios for himself and his wife.

A four-foot-square lantern hangs above the drawing table; sunlight paints plain walls and stained wood. The door behind the lamp displays ornamental framing. A visible post-and-beam structural system orders the studio.

The floor plan, skewed on the diagonal, is unlike any other of Jones's buildings.

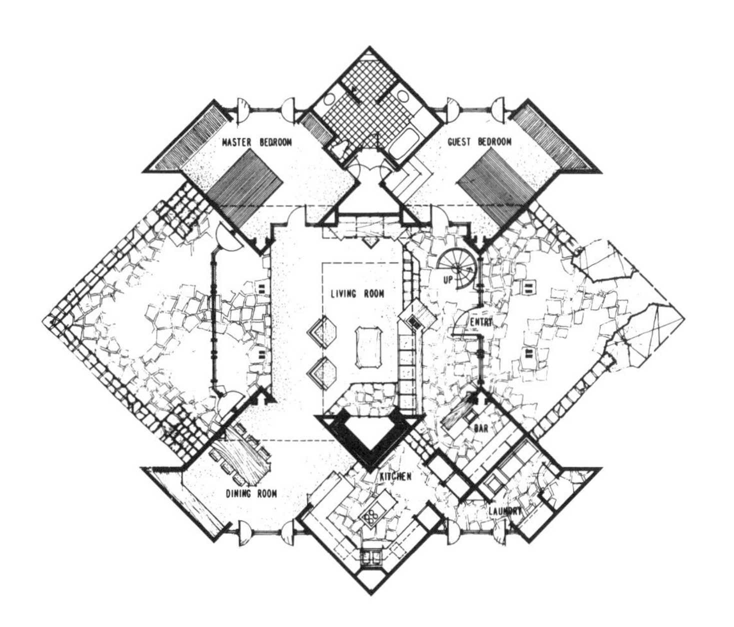

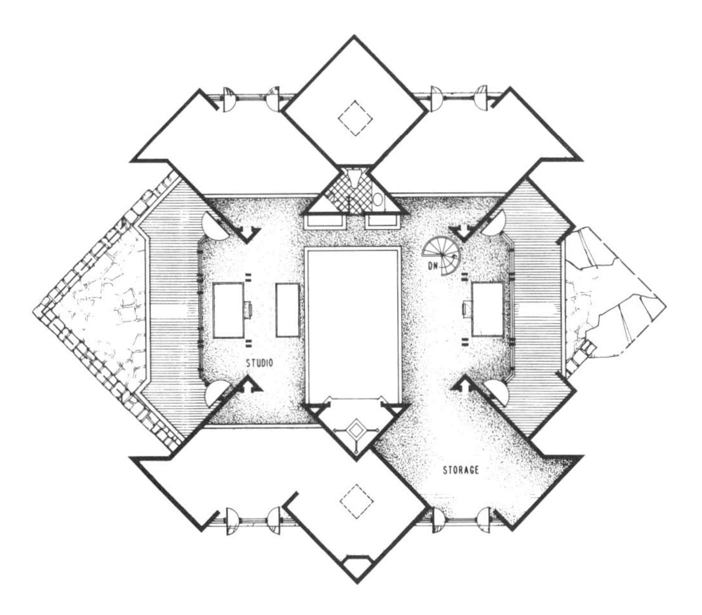

Clerestory light floods the upper reaches above the living room. Continuous beams stabilize the bracing, which drops to flank the angular chimney.

Catwalk, shown above, separates dining area, with its louvered ladderback chairs and oak table, from the living area.

Left: The smooth cast-concrete chimney ascends into the tower, lending substance to a soaring space.

Extended roof planes brace twin towers and provide clerestory lighting.

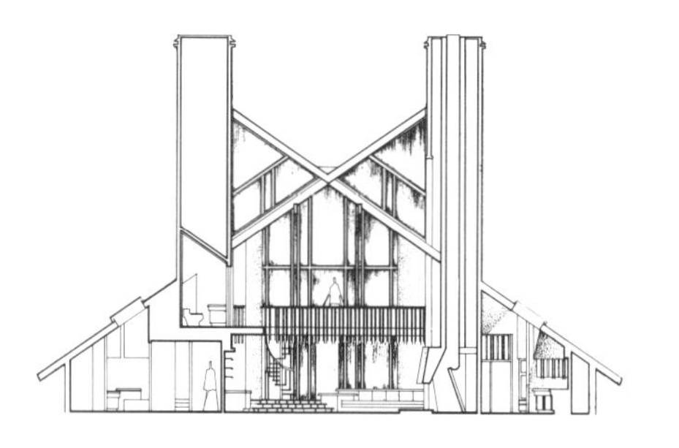

FAIRFIELD BAY, ARKANSAS
1986

Set in the dark green pines above Greer's Ferry Lake at Fairfield Bay, Arkansas, the Norman L. Watson house exhibits Fay Jones's shining high craftsmanship: the site, the residence, and its details combine into a single piece of joinery, a harmoniously dovetailed design. Construction on the retired Amoco executive's residence, which began in October 1983 and ended thirty-three months later, resulted in a building tailored to the owners' wishes.

The Watsons sought comfort and attention to detail in their retirement home, not pretension. From curbside the house seems to be a modest Arkansas chalet with pitched shake roofs, wood batten siding, and a big carport. The visible gable, however, is only the tip of a 6,000-square-foot house that steps down and across a hillside, sheltering spaces both soaring and intimate.

The massive, pitched carport roof exemplifies Jones's affinity for a whole/part relationship in his work. In order to span the distance from high ridge to ground-level wall, the architect devised a series of sculptural steel brackets that carry the weight of the pencil-thin roof.

Unimpeded interior space shifts from outdoor terraces and the entryway to the living room and the master bedroom. Only a small service space is enclosed by doors. Red oak warms the interiors; a massive chimney and fieldstone columns deliberately interrupt the openness. Wood, glass, metal, and mirrors, in combination with silk fabric and the changing light and color of the Arkansas day, are the chief ornamental elements. Nothing seems extraneous.

Invisible, but underpinning the design, is Jones's and partner Maurice Jennings's responsive relationship with their clientele. The firm tailored pragmatic, customized elements for the Watsons, including cabinet doors with hefty strips of red oak along their edges as handles and stiffeners, a folding wood privacy screen that can be opened to bring the living room's sunshine into the master bedroom, and a built-in sofa that doubles as both cabinet and living room wall.

Cabinet stiffeners and privacy screens appear in most of Jones's houses. Rather than devising novel solutions for each design, Jones sees his task as building upon a continuum, exploring the variations possible in a few ideas and a few building types. Neither an imposed solution nor a formal breakthrough, the Watson house represents a refinement of the Greene brothers' tradition of warm, personalized cabinetry bound in Jones's spatially sophisticated frame.

The sawtooth roof extends up the slope to form a car shelter at this Ozark chalet.

The Watson house steps out among dark pines toward Greer's Ferry Lake.

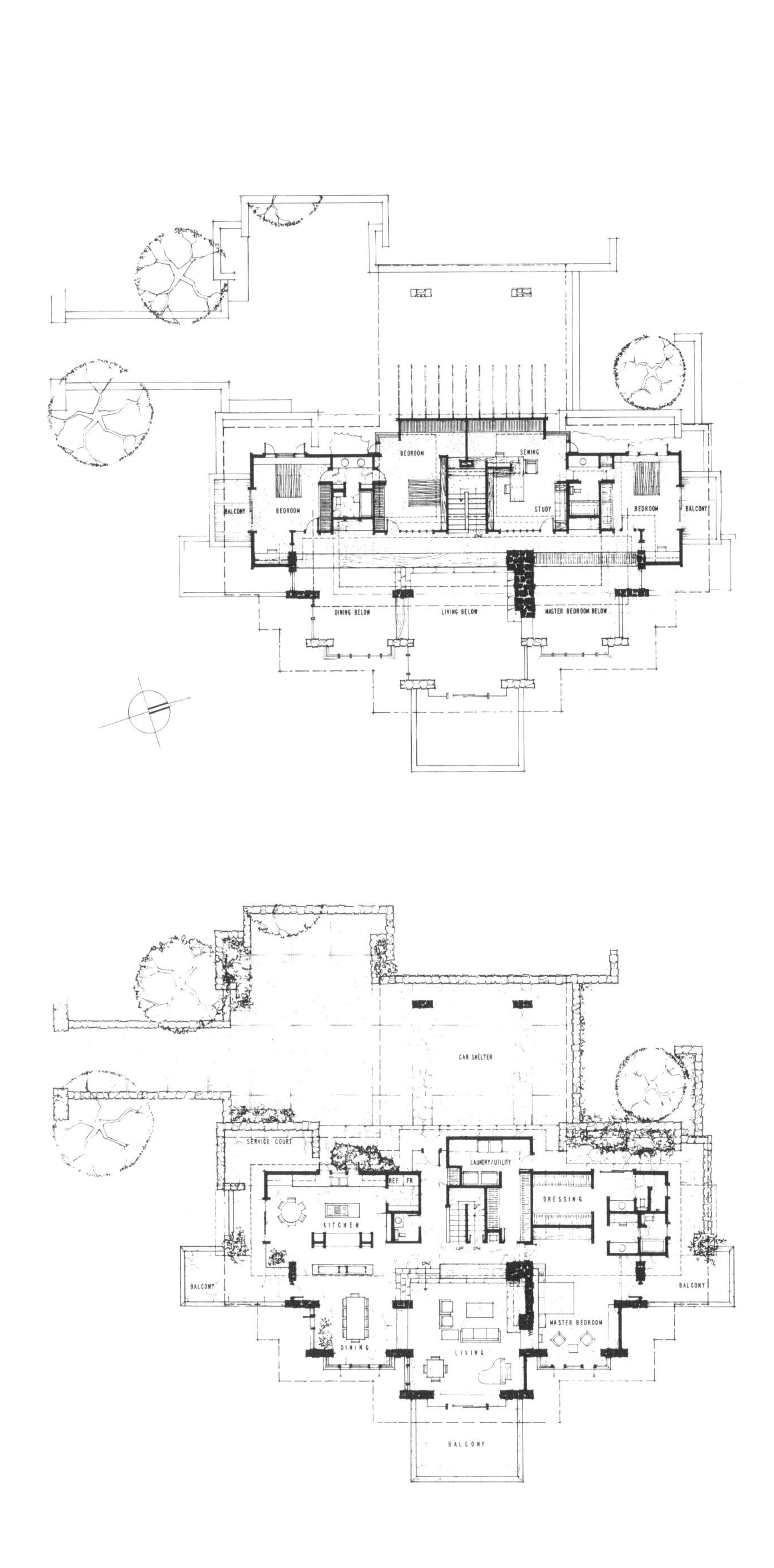
BALCONY
BEDROOM
BEDROOM
SEWING
STUDY
BEDROOM
BALCONY
DINING BELOW
LIVING BELOW
MASTER BEDROOM BELOW
CAR SHELTER
SERVICE COURT
LAUNDRY/UTILITY
REF FR
KITCHEN
DRESSING
BALCONY
BALCONY
DINING
LIVING
MASTER BEDROOM
BALCONY

The broad mass of the three-story, 6,000-square-foot house is hidden from the street. The plan shows a long balcony/bedroom hallway, which opens from the upper floor below to living space. A circulation spine divides the main level; the living spaces step toward the lake.

Above: Metal brackets under the car shelter "allow the roof to remain thinner," says the architect.

Fieldstone columns and chimney, laid with superb craftsmanship, regulate an expansive interior. Circulation follows upper and lower horizontal pathways.

Paired muntins at the clerestory window add rhythm to a balcony passage. The building's thirty-foot chimney required a massive lintel—a seven and a half ton native boulder—chosen jointly by the owners and the architect.

A large dining room lantern, composed of thin oak strips, achieves the lightness of balsa.

I would have to say that Fay Jones is the best architect in the world for what I like: the use of materials, texture, nature, and feeling.

THOMAS S. MONAGHAN, 1991

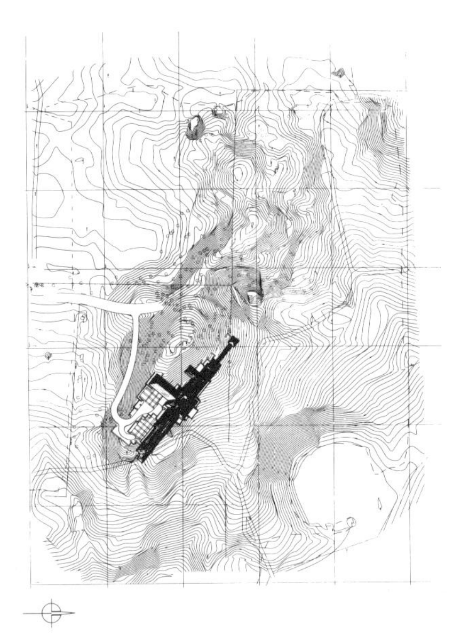

Not all of Jones's designs are built as initially designed. Unbuilt dreams, whether models or drawings, line the shelves of his office on Dickson Street, witnesses of blustering economic winds, of divorce, of new perspectives.

Some clients change their minds. Tom Monaghan, founder of the Domino's Pizza chain and an aficionado of Frank Lloyd Wright's architecture, began the planning for his own home, what he wanted to be "a great piece of residential architecture—the house of houses," by choosing Fay Jones. "It wasn't a tough decision," says Monaghan. "I had been admiring his work for thirty years."

The original plans for Monaghan's residence, part of Domino's larger compound in Ann Arbor, called for a 52,000 square foot house that was reduced through time to 18,000 square feet: still a large house, "hard to keep houselike," according to Jones. Included in its plan were a commercially sized kitchen and a playroom for grandchildren that Monaghan dubbed a "Fantasy kingdom—22 feet tall, with tiered balconies."

Monaghan participated in the programming and design more actively than is typical of Jones's clients. Monaghan offered him "graphic clues by sketching certain ideas," Jones explains. Yet throughout the planning, the client allowed his architect a certain freedom that produced a design with real kinship to Wright "yet not derivative of Wright," the architect feels.

Monaghan had a change of heart that began with the commencement of construction, "when the branch of a massive tree was cut. It almost killed me then." And although the stone foundation of the large house was finally built and the roof partially framed, reading C. S. Lewis's *Mere Christianity* confirmed Monaghan's decision to stop the construction and rethink the house "that was taking over my life."

Subsequently, Jones and Jennings suggested changes to reduce the building's cost, including reduction of building size and substitution of less expensive materials for premium wood and stone (cedar shakes for thick Vermont slate roofing, for example). When confronted with the reality of his compromised plans, that he would not build "the house of houses," Monaghan expressed his frustration: This is going to be just *another* Fay Jones house." Jones's spare retort hit its mark: "What's wrong with that?" As of spring 1992, Monaghan planned to resume construction of the simplified scheme.

ANN ARBOR, MICHIGAN
UNDER CONSTRUCTION, 1992

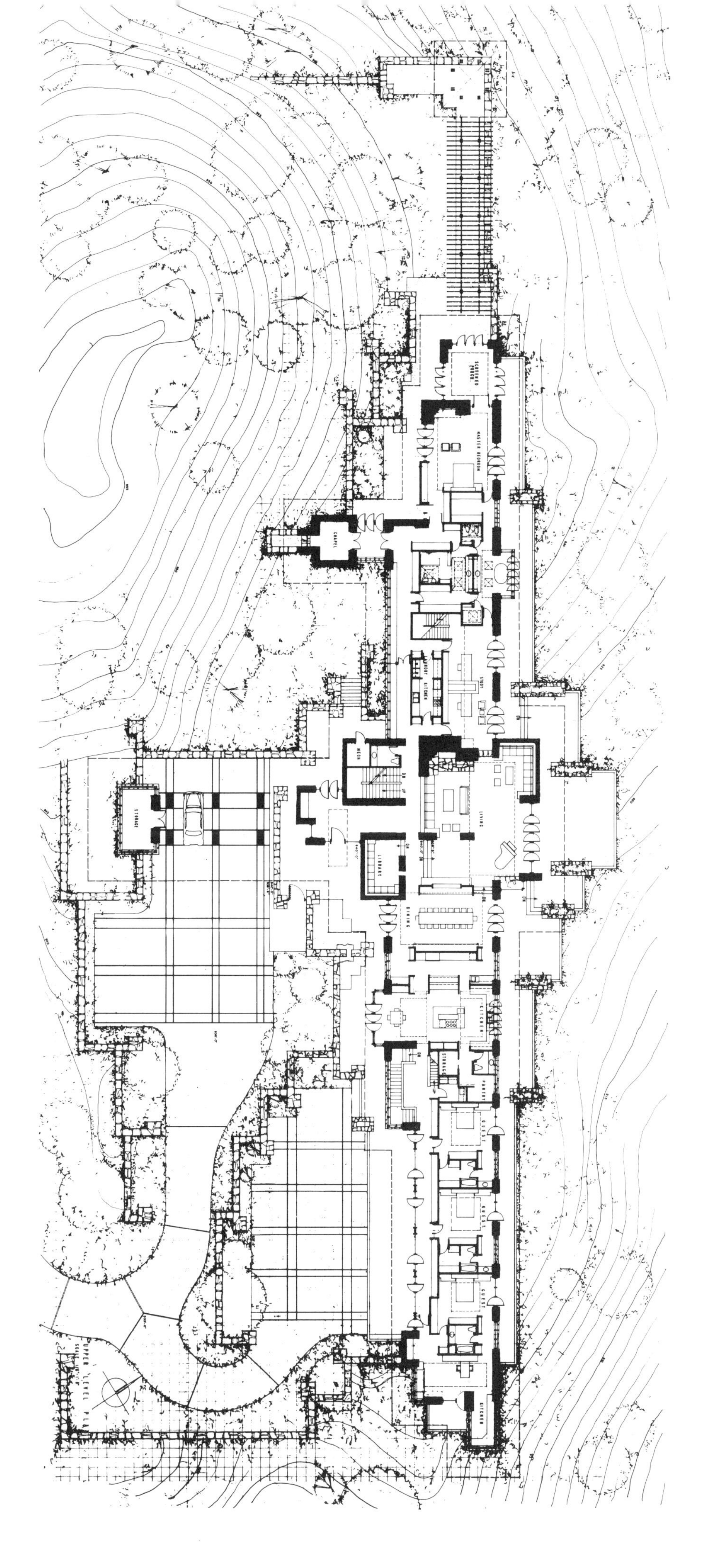

A long spine crowns the ridge. Like a notched stick, the plan stretches along a single line with intersecting wings. This plan, reduced to 18,000 square feet, included multiple kitchens, a chapel, and entertaining areas for large groups.

Perspective drawings offer Wrightian flavor, while the model photographs (above) disclose the scale and further articulate massing and materials hinted at in the drawings.

The lower level plan shares affinity with earlier Jones houses such as Raheen. The building unfolds outwardly, organically.

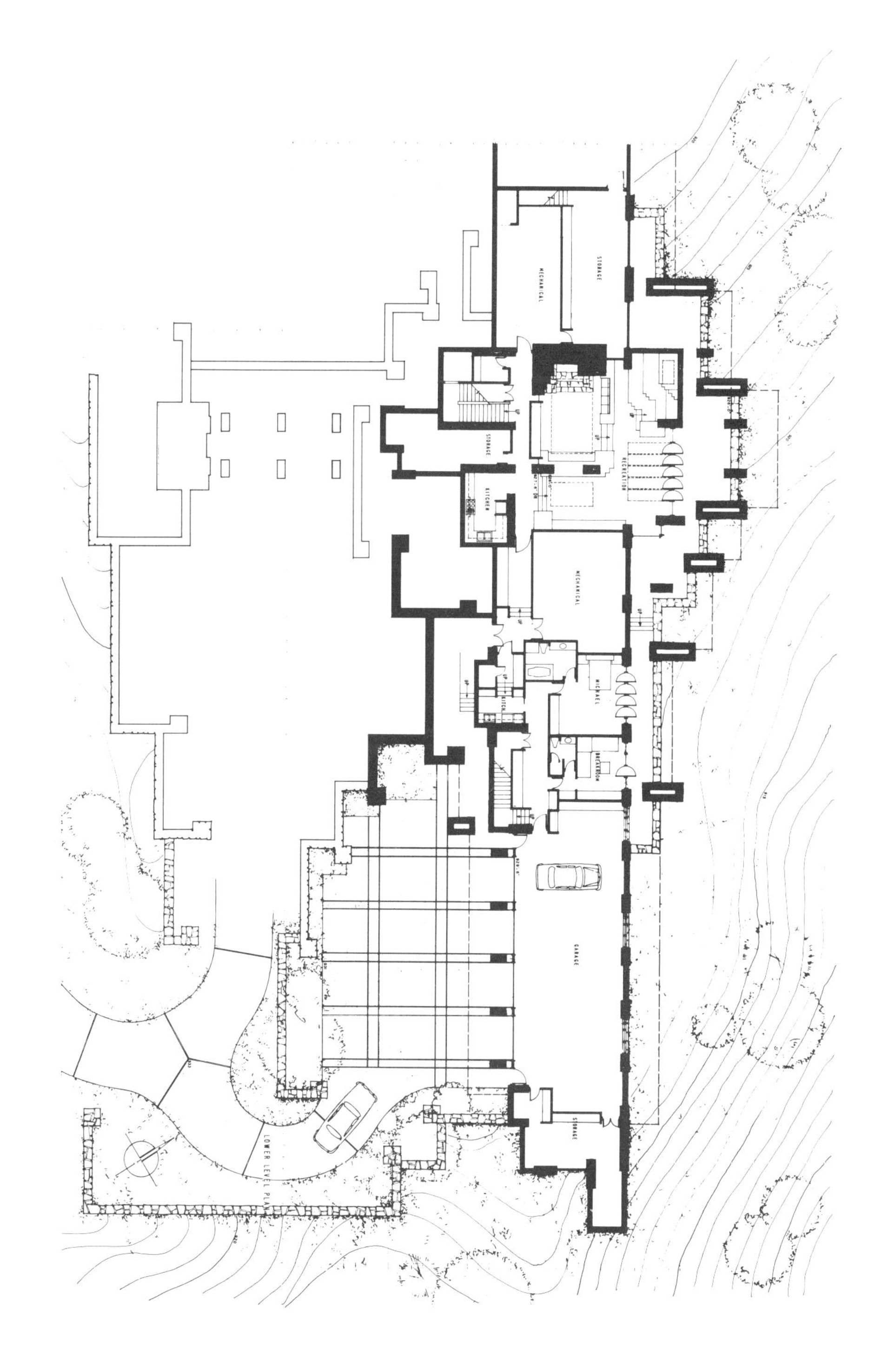

DESIGN OF HOUSES

Orchestrated space—intangible, unphotographable, multidimensional—surrounds and fills Fay Jones's early houses. Although Jones has achieved his own artistic signature, both Jones and Wright share the centrality of space as a design element. In Jones's work, residential landscapes and interiors merge in unity with nature; modulated spaces fuse place and time.

The architect placed early residences on Arkansas' precipitate slopes to provide a sequence of memorable spatial experiences from curbside to hearth. Rarely does a visitor enter a Jones building directly from the street. Earlier architects, from the craftsmen through Wright and the Prairie School, developed the pattern: a meandering path, a covered trellis, or columned promenade beneath an overhanging roof provides protection, shade, and inward focus; each element also frames views out toward the landscape.

Sloping lots frequently mask the houses' true scale; the buildings' height and massing, split to engage a staggered site, are evident only from the rear elevation. Horizontal roofs block expanding horizons and capture hillside space; arcs of evergreens or oaks form woodland clearings for living compounds. Large, roofed courts double as carports and as entertaining shelters. Low masonry walls draw lines in the landscape to refine contours, outline pathways, and define exterior space.

For suburban lots, which typified his early commissions, or for small estates down curving drives, Jones announces the entry with a symbol. A signatory metal lantern, sculpture, or swinging gate identifies the homeowner and the architect. The path then proceeds inward to the embracing composition.

Discoveries abound along the way, from small fountains to passage beneath greenhouse canopies. Small open-air courts in the Japanese manner, whether passive spaces meant for viewing or active ones to be entered, surround Jones's houses. Decks, cantilevered or columned, yield outdoor perches for sleeping and sitting.

An illusory continuity binds indoors and out. Windows provide transparent barriers between heated spaces and the out-of-doors. Large glass sheets set directly in stone flooring become invisible when bordered by pachysandra or ground ivy. Without traditional frames, mullions, and sills, the line between outdoors and indoors evaporates.

Jones's ability to control space, while distinct from his mentor's, recalls Wright's. While Jones's concern for structural expression is manifest in early buildings, his first residential essays echo

Wright's use of wall, floor, and ceiling planes to define interactive interior volumes.

In the early houses, the connection between both architects is particularly clear: Wrightian space flows like water. Variations in ceiling configuration and pitch, from steep gables to lowered, coffered trays, enrich spatial variety, as the Henley house in El Dorado illustrates. Steps up to dining areas or down to living rooms tighten or expand the volume. Furnishings and art objects bring scale to soaring interiors; built-in cabinetry punctuates the interior spatial flow.

Clerestory windows and skylights heighten the continuity; glass doors, which open to gardens, light, and air, extend horizontal axes. Mirrors, undifferentiated from windows on high end walls, extend apparent depth; opposed corner mirrors seem to negate the buildings' structure.

Unfolding, interrelated spaces hold mystery and promise: what lies around the next corner, behind a column, or within a recess? Dynamism, an energy derived from the arrangement of juxtaposed, varied volumes, enlivens each house and each landscape. The essence of each residence is revealed slowly, however. Only moving through the houses or living in them confirms Jones's spatial mastery. Fay Jones's houses are not merely objects meant for viewing, but are intended as complex vessels for human experience. ▲

Henley Residence
El Dorado, Arkansas
1960

I depend heavily on the craftsmen—those who build, those who give their skill.

FAY JONES

As the first buildings and sites testify, Jones found his voice early; materials provided a vocabulary. Jones sought to employ them "according to nature. If you are using brick, then it needs to do what brick does best." Like other practitioners in the organic tradition, he still seeks an understanding of each material, not only how it looks, but how it acts; how it bears structural loads, individually and in concert with other members; how it is best joined to similar and dissimilar building elements; and what effect it will have on the total building.

Consider stone. The stone Jones uses is an Arkansas native, usually a fieldstone from a nearby quarry, sometimes from a dismantled stone fence. The frequent use of wood and stone has prompted others to label Jones's work an "Ozark style." However, the architect deploys these strong, indigenous materials, extracted from North America's oldest mountains, with more sophistication than the rustic epithet implies.

James Residence
Ruston, Louisiana
1978

Consider wood. Jones admits that although he tried to purchase native species for early projects, their higher cost prompted him to visit the commercial lumberyard for "store bought." Today, he employs a range of woods, but maintains a consistency in their use. An entire building, for example, may be faced with western red cedar, while interior woodwork is fir plywood. Wood choices depend on applications: redwood and cedar for exterior walls, cedar shakes for roofs, strip oak for floors, and, for millwork, fir or birch plywood ranging up to fine oak, mahogany, and cherry.

Other materials include brick, which when used instead of stone, results in a more cleanly defined geometry. Stucco increases contrast between wall and forest; its smooth planes highlight wood detailing. Sheet glass is a major wall component in all the residences.

Thin steel acts in concert with other materials, supporting exterior eaves or interior beams in repetitious, ornamental bracketing, or alone, perhaps as a garden ornament or a property sign. Concrete's plastic quality is sometimes molded into a chimney, dam, or weir.

Inside a Jones house, carpet frequently covers what stone, vinyl, or wood flooring does not, juxtaposing soft and hard materials. Countertops are laminated plastic, dressed stone, or sheets of stainless steel. Cork may sheathe walls, allowing the simple mounting of artwork. Upholstery and draperies frequently are muted raw silk or wool; accent pieces may be covered in brighter fabrics. From steel to stone, care in craftsmanship plays a large part in making a Jones house, even in the construction of gypsum board walls. In order to get a true surface from irregular lumber, the architects insist that carpenters rip all 2 x 12 rafters down to a consistent plane. "There is no rough carpentry in any of our projects," says Jones's partner, Maurice Jennings.

Jones and Jennings keep costs down by devising details that can be built with ordinary hand tools. For one of Jones's first commissions he designed an ornamental wood lantern from plywood. The laminated wood was scored by parallel cuts from a table saw. Grooves vented heat from the fixture while allowing light from the lantern to glow outward.

A similar utility and ease of construction distinguish custom furniture designed by the Fayetteville firm. Ottoman cushions are lifted to reveal simple plywood boxes that are easy to build and useful for storage. Many items of furniture serve more than one function. The back of a built-in sofa, for example, may function simultaneously as a low cabinet, room divider, and table.

Jones's houses invite personalization. Unlike chaste, "high-style" interiors, the warm woods and natural fabrics lend an air of domestic comfort and provide a setting for the owners' art and other objects. High shelves, meant for a collection of porcelain, surround the dining space at Pine Knoll; built-in library shelving displays artwork, books, and family photography. Most millwork is built-in.

From the earliest days of his practice, Jones has cultivated a cadre of Arkansas workers—stonemasons, woodworkers, and welders—who regularly execute his office's designs. Jimmy Price, a metalworker, maintains a shop in Fayetteville where Jones's elaborate brackets and sculptures hang from cranes beside auto bodies. Junior Treece, an Arkansas woodcrafter, fabricates doors, windows, and furniture. Jones and Jennings are champions of local talent, but they find good craftspeople wherever a project may be in the United States, although usually at higher cost than in Arkansas. ◬

Ornamentation is wrought in the warp and woof of the structure. It is constitutional in the best sense.

FRANK LLOYD WRIGHT
In the Cause of Architecture

Jones draws upon his early engineering training to design structures grounded in science, informed by history, and infused with lyricism. When all the pieces fit, Jones's structural expressionism makes habitable sculpture.

Jones's foundation systems seem apt for each site; they are never imposed. For rocky hillsides, Jones employs naturalistic rock walls as the base of tree-tall, wooden superstructures. Ashlar foundations in finely laid ribbons extend horizontally at hilltop houses like Pine Knoll, to emphasize solidity and rest. Where sites are extreme, on the sides of bluffs or in the water, the architect cantilevers decks into the air or bridges streams.

He showed his engineering penchant in the early residences, which expose substantial structural systems to view. Three or four primary, longitudinal beams support the gable roofs. Typically, the beams lie slightly down the roof from the ridgeline for emphasis. As the Greene brothers did, Jones extends the supporting framework beyond the gable roofs. Inside, ridge beams rest on wood posts or stone columns; outside, the same long beams continue past overhanging roofs.

Beginning in his early houses, like the Parsons house at Springdale, Arkansas, Jones uses wall and ceiling framing as an integral, ornamental device. When asked about the relationship of ornament to structure, Jones explains: "It is the integration of these things that gives the fullest meaning. They are part and parcel of the same thing.

Unlike Wright, a structural pioneer, Jones has limited his range; most of Jones's work employs the simple post and beam. The integrated structural patterns he discovered such as cross-bracing have evolved into sculpture. While he stops short of calling his own work beautiful, he acknowledges "the underlying order that people seem to respond to." Jones has opened a door to deeper exploration of structure, structure's relation to ornament, and ornament's power within human consciousness.

Jones melds ornament into the overall design and into structure with assurance. Like Wright, Jones employs ornamental motifs as formal manifestations of underlying structural or functional necessity. Faced with a need, reason ignites an idea that Jones then pursues, embellishes, and integrates into the entire building.

Sometimes the rationale for ornament lies hidden from sight. "Some of the more intricate work that looks like pure decoration does serve more purpose than just as some kind of ornamentation or adornment," Jones says. For example, wood mullions in window screens at Stonelodge continue geometric patterns present throughout the residence; yet they also brace each door structurally while they prevent the tearing of the metal fabric.

The word "pattern" is operative. Jones mentions a "basic pattern, a geometric theme" that comes into play in large and small elements in his houses. His design method, he explains, makes pattern the manifestation of a "theme in all parts . . . an essential essence, an essential character . . . some kind of seed at the core." Patterns occur in both the overall design and in the microcosm.

Alone, the individual thematic decorative elements might seem trivial. Single pieces, their geometric qualities considered separately, lack the resonance they possess as parts of a larger pattern. When considered in the ensemble, they strengthen the whole/part relationship—they are, in Jones's word, "accompaniment" to the "all-encompassing theme."

Parsons Residence
Springdale, Arkansas
1966

Snow Residence
Fayetteville, Arkansas
1962

Unlike hermetically sealed contemporary buildings, earth, fire, wind, and water are nearby in Jones's houses. The interrelationship of sensory experiences associated with these elements, whether touch, sight, smell, or hearing, gives each building its nuances. None is more crucial to his architecture than the concomitant of fire—light.

Light is energy. As Jones's early Arkansas houses illustrate, he understands light's ability to transform interiors, to suffuse space with life, and to highlight texture, color, and form. Daylight is his primary power source. Before opening a wall with glass, Jones carefully studies its orientation and considers how topography and vegetation affect living spaces.

Controlled eastern sunlight, filtered through the tree canopy, awakens dining and living spaces; overhanging roofs shade south-facing glass. Infrequently used spaces, such as storage rooms or baths, are strung along western walls to block extreme summer heat.

Skylights crown most residences, filling the spaces with a light similar to that in a museum. Daylight from above intensifies the three-dimensionality of objects within and without. Light from

a high source points up texture on stone chimney walls, emphasizes height and verticality, displays pattern in structure and ornament, and, as the sun moves across the sky, brings motion into otherwise still spaces.

Day differs from night inside glass walls, an effect Jones exploits: windows opening to fields and sky become opaque sheltering walls that reflect artificial illumination at night. Incandescent warmth extends from nighttime interiors outdoors onto patios and decks, where lamps define walkways and seating areas.

Jones never reveals an artificial light's source; concealed and baffled, illumination fills a space indirectly. Continuous coves of incandescent light wash living spaces. Light seeps through fabric screens or cuts through wooden baffles to create shadowed pattern on ceilings or walls. Massive lanterns illuminate the spot for eating or entering. Sculptural wooden lamps shoot light upward and downward, creating puddles of light. No harsh light source overwhelms the calm spaces.

Pools of water reinforce the peaceful settings. Of the ancient elements, water touches deepest, to evoke emotion, healing, and peace, and as in myth, sleep and memory. Jones understands water's power to alter moods, whether in running streams, dammed ponds, or still interior pools and fountains. He never hesitates to modify nature with concrete dams or weirs. Plants further soothe the psyche. The watery pools that dot the properties are graced with lilies, and the fountains with ferns and sculpture. Waterside plants soften the line between man-made shelter and nature.

Sound flows with moving water; seasons alter its intensity. Full creeks provide constant humming sounds; fall droughts reduce the amplitude to a trickle. Interior fountains splash softly, introducing civilized peace to his sensual houses.

Texture encourages touch, inviting human hands to stroke a wall's rough surface. The range of textures is broad: feathery shake roofs, hard stone walls and chimneys, rough exterior or smooth interior wood walls and millwork, and sharp metal accent pieces.

Pleasant odors pervade the rooms. A redolent earth scent emanates from subterranean exposed rock walls. Pungent cedar, brisk fir, stringent oak and other woods spread their aromas throughout the houses. Near the hearth's ashes or in the greenhouse, individual odors blend into a potpourri, which may be whisked away momentarily by a fresh breeze.

The type of home that abounds today . . . a type in which practical comfort and art are skillfully wedded—is no architectural pose, no temporary style. It is a vital product of a time, place and people, with roots deep in geographical and human needs. It has a definite relation to the kind of climate and soil, the habits of the people, and their ways of looking at civilization and nature.

The Craftsman, 1912

People delight in recognizing an architectural language established by repetition. A Jones composition includes repetition that grows from minor details to large-scale structural systems. Jones interrelates arcaded rows of similar stone columns with exposed, glorified roof framing; non-structural wood battens, repeated at each column point, highlight the ceilings. Geometric design motifs create a unifying symbolic language.

Repetition is reinforced by conformity of parts. At Stoneflower, Jones matches repeated pairings of equally sized columns along opposite walls. He breaks regularity for emphasis, as when he places a massive boulder within the repeated stonework of a chimney.

The repetition of regular pieces based on mathematical models establishes rhythm. A time signature is legible in the placement of building materials at Stoneflower, from reiterated patterns in the strip wood floor, which begin a cadence, to the repeated pattern of wall columnation, to recurrent roof bracing encircling the space.

Symmetry emphasizes order. Axial symmetry characterizes the planning of early houses like Stoneflower, whose entire upper level is a single, lucid room. Cruciform plans balance equally weighted wings. Building sections restate the symmetrical theme. Overhead structure, including outdoor trellises, emphasize regularity by setting a balanced pattern that prepares the visitor for the larger composition.

Although axial symmetry brings order to many of Jones's houses, he often arranges houses asymmetrically and balances the compositions within a larger framework. In his centrifugal floor plans (sometimes called pinwheel plans), spaces spin around a defined central point—often the chimney and hearth. The result is equilibrium, a state of harmony among the parts that suggests wholeness and completeness. It is this sense of balance, as much as any other formal sense, that has evoked admiration from Jones's critics and clients.

In addition to balance, comprehension of placement in space produces a sense of well-being in a Jones house: you know where you are in relation to the overall scheme. Visual axes, sometimes corresponding to circulation patterns, sometimes reaching toward the out-of-doors, set up a strong spatial geometry. On entering Stonelodge, the visitor's eye is drawn to an interior pathway that extends through the building to a patio. The larger living space opens outward on a cross axis that stretches to the blue line of the Ozarks. An apparent rational order provides orientation.

Although Jones minimizes the number of discrete interior spaces in a house, each is placed and defined to mark its relative importance to the overall scheme. As in the Clark residence, living and dining spaces typically share center stage and open to kitchens positioned behind low walls or behind chimneys. Subservient spaces such as laundry or dressing rooms terminate secondary passageways, removed from the central hearth.

Hierarchical planning underscores the sense of place in Jones's axial plans. Changing floor levels signify spatial and functional importance. Sometimes Jones places bedrooms higher than the main living levels; a vertical break in the horizontal flow can mark the entry into a larger and more important space.

All of Jones's buildings share a simplicity produced by a harmonious joinery. He has pared the pieces to the minimum in his more recent work, such as the Reed house and the chapels. But even the earliest houses share an overriding sense of order, a sensory appeal, and flowing spaces marked by works of art and craft.

The Craftsman could have been describing Jones and Jennings's residential work when it described houses in which "practical comfort and art are skillfully wedded." Although intended for our own time and culture, Jones's contemporary houses emerge from "roots deep in geographical and human need," designed for human comfort and shelter, not for show.

Clark Residence
Arkansas
1963

Fay Jones enjoys a loyal clientele. Its numbers have steadily grown since 1956, the year he began to build, through decades of wavering public enthusiasm for architecture and raging professional debate. His small-town architectural practice centered around Fayetteville has spread beyond Arkansas, ultimately stretching from metropolitan Boston to the Colorado Rockies, from Michigan to Mobile Bay.

One magazine article unlocked public enthusiasm. Jones's first published house, the Calvin Bain residence, featured in *House Beautiful* in 1959, resulted in more than 600 unsolicited requests for house plans, according to Gus Jones. As the office manager, she wrote a form letter explaining that no plans were being offered. Requests for plans and services followed each subsequent publication.

Men and women with the assurance of personal achievement seem drawn to Jones's work. A representative list is instructive: entrepreneurs, such as Domino's Pizza founder Tom Monaghan and the late Sam Walton, founder of the Wal-Mart discount chain; former top corporate executives Robert Alexander of Ford Motor Company and Norman Watson of Amoco; writer and former *New York Times* correspondent Roy Reed. And, although National Book Award winner Ellen Gilchrist did not commission the Jones house she lives in, she returned to Fayetteville after a hiatus in the 1980s, in part, she explains, to live in a Fay Jones house.

What has attracted them to Jones? Jones's association with Frank Lloyd Wright spurred Michigan State professors Alma Goetsch and Katherine Winckler to build in Arkansas. Owners of one of Wright's classic Usonian houses of the 1939-40 period, termed Wright's "favorite small house," they retired from Okemos, Michigan, to Fayetteville, another university town. There, in 1968, they built what became Jones's version of the Goetsch-Winkler house, a two-bedroom residence with open studio and living space.

Some found Jones through a third-party referral. Robert Alexander and his wife, visiting their newly purchased farmland near Fayetteville, were introduced to Jones through a local realtor, who described him as a "reasonably good architect in town." A slide show in the architect's office convinced them they had found the right designer. "One thing I have noticed in successful people is their enthusiasm. Fay's enthusiasm is very infectious," Mr. Alexander says.

When Norman Watson of Chicago decided to retire to Fairfield Bay, Arkansas, he relied on advice from his corporation's real estate department, which checked sources in nearby St. Louis. More than a year after the initial meeting, Mrs. Watson learned from Jones's partner that the client's affirmative decision was not the only one to be made, but that Jones "mulls around and decides whom he wants to work with."

Others, like restaurant executive Don Edmondson, had known Jones for years. He explains that he "knew he wanted a house like that" in 1954, when his University of Arkansas professor, Fay Jones, showed slides of Frank Lloyd Wright's work. Having Jones design his house fulfilled a long-held ambition.

Most Jones projects require a year's planning. When the Robert Alexanders returned to Arkansas from England after a year's absence, they had "no idea what we were going to see." They found the architect had "a whole package of drawings. Some were in great detail. We instantly liked it." Their suggestions for changes to the initial design were restricted to the deletion of one bedroom from the scheme.

Other clients report an almost universal satisfaction with the results of their joint planning efforts. The Edmondsons moved one wall a single grid line's distance (two feet eight inches) from where the wall was designated on the original drawings. Helen Walton suggested a small table for her kitchen rather than the long bar-height counter the architect had proposed.

Construction time, depending on a building's complexity, has ranged from eighteen months to three years, as the Watsons' experience illustrates. According to Mr. Watson, "Fay had been thinking about eighteen months to two years to build the house." Thirty-three months elapsed between the first site work and move-in day in July 1986. Watson faults neither the architect nor the builders, saying of the latter, "They were perfectionists themselves; they worked nine-hour days to make sure it was done correctly."

When clients are paying contractors by the hour, as Watson did, an extended construction schedule for customizing detail work can increase a project's cost. A former accountant, Mr. Watson kept his own books and witnessed rising material costs as his own house was under construction. He describes Jones and partner Jennings as "very interested in anything that would save money," including their reliance on local sources for resources such as stone.

Jones remains protective of his clients' budgets but offers that he has built houses in a wide range, extending from $10 per square foot (in the late 1950s) to more than ten times that amount in recent years. Not all of Jones's contemporary buildings come at high cost. Thorncrown Chapel's total cost was "over $200,000," says Mrs. James Reed, wife of the commissioning client, who adds that an appraisal conducted two years after its completion valued the building at $500,000.

Many of Jones's clients mention his firm's thorough assistance throughout the construction period. Norman Watson describes Jones's ingenuity when confronted with a problem: "The builders reported that two sheets of glass exceeded 130 inches in length, which approximately doubled the cost of this glazing. I reported it to Fay, and I let him alone—let him do his work. He came back with three excellent options." As built, the tall windows are trimmed sympathetically with wood at rail height, and the cost was slashed.

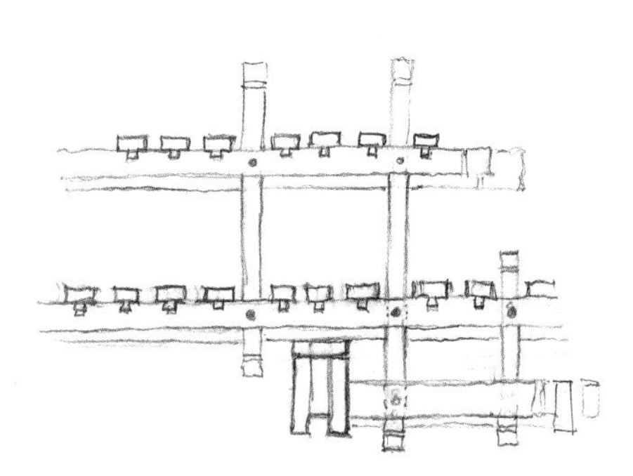

Preliminary sketch for a terrace trellis, Edmondson Residence.

The Jones/Jennings relationship with their clients extends beyond the construction period. The Edmondson house stretched into an eight-year project as the family grew and a guest house was added. Watson appreciates that Jones and Jennings "like to follow up as you consider further changes down the line." He and his wife express the experience of many other clients when they say Jones and Jennings have become lifetime friends.

REPRESENTATIVE PROJECT LIST

1955
Jones Residence
E. Fay Jones, Fayetteville, Arkansas

1958
Bain Residence
Calvin Bain, Prairie Grove, Arkansas

1960
Fletcher Residence
Adrian Fletcher, Fayetteville, Arkansas

Henley Residence
Paul Henley, El Dorado, Arkansas

Walton Residence
Sam Walton, Arkansas

1962
Hunter Residence
Sam Hunter, Memphis, Tennessee

Snow Residence
Blanche Snow, Fayetteville, Arkansas

1963
Clark Residence
Maxine and Joseph Marsh Clark, Arkansas

Demarco Residence
Norman Demarco, Fayetteville, Arkansas

Nance Residence
Joe Nance, Harrison, Arkansas

Smith Residence
Rex Smith, Fayetteville, Arkansas

Stonelodge
Earl Lane, Hot Springs, Arkansas

1964 *Faubus Residence*
Hon. Orval Faubus, Huntsville, Arkansas

Pine Knoll
Graham Hall, Little Rock, Arkansas
Current Owner: Chuck and Margaret Ensminger

1965 *Stoneflower*
Robert Shaheen and Curt Goodfellow, Eden Isle, Arkansas
Current Owner: H.F. Falbaum

Underwood Building
Bill Underwood, Fayetteville, Arkansas

1966 *Applegate Residence*
Joe Applegate, Bentonville, Arkansas

Parsons Residence
Glenn Parsons, Springdale, Arkansas

1967 *Cheatham Residence*
Phil Cheatham, Memphis, Tennessee

1968 *Goetsch-Winckler Residence*
Alma Goetsch and Katherine Winckler, Fayetteville, Arkansas

1969 *Eaglehead Conference Center*
Lake Lingamore, Maryland

1970 *Gazebo*
North Little Rock, Arkansas

1974 *McNamee Residence*
William McNamee, Clarksdale, Mississippi

1975 *Raheen*
Alice and Bob Alexander, outside Fayetteville, Arkansas

1976 *Broyles Residence*
Frank Broyles, Fayetteville, Arkansas

Ney Residence
Randolph J. Ney, Fort Smith, Arkansas

1977 *Pallone Residence*
Sam Pallone, outside Little Rock, Arkansas
Current Owner: Lila and Jack Riggs

1978 *James Residence*
Robbie James, Ruston, Louisiana

Lutz Residence
Tom Lutz, Shell Knob, Missouri

1979 *East Residence*
Don East, Tulsa, Oklahoma

1980 *Hotz Residence*
Hartman Hotz, Fayetteville, Arkansas

	Thorncrown Chapel James Reed, Eureka Springs, Arkansas
1983	*Edmondson Residence* Don and Ellen Edmondson, Forrest City, Arkansas
	Reed Residence Roy Reed, Hogeye, Arkansas
1984	*Davenport Residence* Lawrence Davenport, Evergreen, Colorado
1986	*Watson Residence* Norman L. Watson, Fairfield Bay, Arkansas
1987	*Grober Residence* Jack Grober, Fort Smith, Arkansas
	Pinecote Pavilion (The Native Plant Center of the Crosby Arboretum) The Crosby Arboretum, Picayune, Mississippi
1988	*Mildred B. Cooper Memorial Chapel* Bella Vista, Arkansas
	Wilhelm Residence Weston Wilhelm, Hilton Head, South Carolina
1989	*Richardson Residence* Fontaine Richardson, Carlyle, Massachusetts
	Thorncrown Worship Center James Reed, Eureka Springs, Arkansas
1990	*Marty Leonard Community Chapel* Lena Pope Home, Fort Worth, Texas
	Monaghan Residence (under construction, 1992) Thomas S. Monaghan, Ann Arbor, Michigan
	Nelms Residence Don Nelms, Fayetteville, Arkansas
	Pederson Residence George Pederson, McLean, Virginia
	Yarbrough Residence Clark Yarbrough, Montrose, Alabama

HONORS

American Institute of Architects (AIA)
"Homes for Better Living" Award, with the cooperation of:
Life and *House and Home* magazines, 1961;
The American Home and *House and Home* magazines, 1964;
The American Home and *House and Home* magazines, 1966;
Housing magazine, 1978

Honor Award: Fletcher Residence, 1961; Walton Residence, 1961;
Thorncrown Chapel, 1981; Reed House, 1987; Pinecote Pavilion, 1990

Award of Merit: Snow Residence, 1964; Stoneflower, 1966;
Pallone Residence, 1978

Gold Medal, 1990

American Institute of Steel Construction
Architectural Award of Excellence, 1973: Gazebo, North Little Rock, Arkansas

American Plywood Association
Design Awards Program, Citation, 1977

American Wood Council
National Design Award: Thorncrown Chapel, 1981; Pinecote Pavilion, 1987

Architectural Record
"Record Houses," 1978: Pallone Residence

Building Stone Institute
Tucker Architectural Award for Design Excellence, 1981:
Raheen, Thorncrown Chapel

Progressive Architecture Design Awards
Citation, 1967: Friedman Residence

Red Cedar Shingle & Handsplit Shake Bureau (with the AIA)
First Award: Reed Residence, 1983; Raheen, 1984; Pinecote Pavilion, 1987

Tau Sigma Delta
Gold Medal for Distinction in Architectural Design, 1984

STATE AND REGIONAL ARCHITECTURAL AWARDS

Arkansas Chapter, AIA
Honor Award: Pallone Residence, 1978; Thorncrown Chapel, 1980;
Raheen, 1980; Carver Residence, 1980; Lutz Residence, 1980

Gold Medal, 1986

Gulf States Region, AIA
Honor Award: Pallone Residence, 1979; Reed Residence, 1983;
Edmondson Residence, 1983; Pinecote Pavilion, 1987

Award for Excellence: Thorncrown Chapel, 1980; Raheen, 1980

ACADEMIC ACHIEVEMENT

EDUCATION

1950 University of Arkansas, Bachelor in Architecture

1951 Rice University, Master in Architecture

1953 Taliesin Fellowship, Apprenticeship to Frank Lloyd Wright

ACADEMIC DISTINCTION

1950-51 Fellowship in Architecture
Rice University

1961 Distinguished Faculty Award
University of Arkansas

Faculty Distinguished Achievement Award in Research
University of Arkansas Alumni Association

1976 Architecture Distinguished Alumnus Award
University of Arkansas

1980-81 Rome Prize Fellowship/Mid-Career Fellowship in Architecture and Design
American Academy in Rome with National Endowment for the Arts

1981 Distinguished Alumnus Citation
University of Arkansas

1982 Faculty Distinguished Achievement Award in Research
University of Arkansas Alumni Association

1984 Honorary Doctorate of Fine Arts
Kansas State University

1985 ACSA Distinguished Professor Award
Association of Collegiate Schools of Architecture

Honorary Doctorate of Humanities
Drury College

1989 Distinguished Alumnus Award
Rice University

1990 Honorary Doctorate of Humane Letters
Hendrix College

Honorary Doctorate in Arts and Humane Letters
University of Arkansas

BOOKS

Andrew, David Stephen. "Louis Sullivan and the Problem of Meaning in Architecture." Ph.D. diss., Washington University, St. Louis, 1979.

Canty, Donald, ed. *The Annual of American Architecture–1981*. Washington: American Institute of Architects, 1981.

Catanese, Anthony J., and James C. Snyder. *Introduction to Architecture.* New York: McGraw-Hill, 1979.

Doremus, Thomas. *Frank Lloyd Wright and Le Corbusier: The Great Dialogue.* New York: Van Nostrand Reinhold, 1985.

Drexler, Arthur. *The Drawings of Frank Lloyd Wright.* New York: Horizon, 1962.

Drexler, Arthur, and Thomas S. Hines. *The Architecture of Richard Neutra: From International Style to California Modern.* New York: Museum of Modern Art, 1982.

Egbert, Donald Drew. "The Idea of Organic Experimentation and American Architecture." In *Evolutionary Thought in America*, edited by Stow Persons for Princeton University program on American civilization. New Haven: Yale University Press, 1950.

Frampton, Kenneth. *Modern Architecture–1920–1945*. New York: Rizzoli, 1983.

——. *Modern Architecture–1851–1919.* New York: Oxford University Press, 1983.

——. *Modern Architecture: A Critical History.* New York: Oxford University Press, 1980.

Germany, Lisa. *Harwell Hamilton Harris* (exhibit catalog). Austin: University of Texas Center for the Study of American Architecture, 1985.

Hines, Thomas S. *Richard Neutra and the Search for Modern Architecture.* New York: Oxford University Press, 1982.

Kennedy, Roger G. *American Churches.* New York: Stewart, Tabori & Chang, 1982.

Makinson, Randall L. *Greene & Greene–Architecture as a Fine Art.* Salt Lake City: Peregrine Smith, 1977.

McCoy, Esther. *Five California Architects.* New York: Praeger, 1975.

Moholy-Nagy, L., and Walter Gropius, eds. *The New Vision: Fundamentals of Design, Painting, Sculpture, Architecture.* New York: W.W. Norton, 1935.

Neutra, Richard. *Life and Shape.* New York: Appleton-Century Crofts, 1962.

Plummer, Henry. *The Potential House.* Tokyo: A + U Printing Co., 1989.

Sullivan, Louis H. *A System of Architectural Ornament ACCD with a Philosophy of Man's Powers.* Washington: American Institute of Architects, 1924. Reprint. New York: Eakins, 1967.

——. *Autobiography of an Idea.* Reprint. New York: Dover, 1956.

——. *Democracy: A Man Search.* Circa 1961. Westport, Conn.: Greenwood, 1973.

——. "Emotional Architecture as Compared with Classical." In *American Architectural Books* (based on H. R. Hitchcock bibliography of the same title). New Haven: Resource, 1972.

——. *Kindergarten Chats & Other Writings.* Revised 1918. New York: G. Wittenborn, circa 1947.

——. *The Testament of Stone: Themes of Idealism and Indignation from the Writings of Louis Sullivan.* Edited by Maurice English. Evanston, Ill.: Northwestern University Press, 1963.

Wright, Frank Lloyd. *An Autobiography.* New York: Horizon, circa 1977.

——. *An Organic Architecture: The Architecture of Democracy.* Circa 1939. Reprint. Cambridge, Mass.: MIT Press, 1970.

——. *Frank Lloyd Wright on Architecture: Selected Writings, 1894–1940.* Edited by Frederick Gutheim. New York: Duell, Sloan & Pearce, 1941.

——. *Modern Architecture: Being the Kahn Lectures for 1930.* Published for the Department of Art and Archeology of Princeton. Princeton: Princeton University Press, 1931.

——. *A Testament.* New York: Horizon, 1957.

——. *The Natural House.* New York: Horizon, 1954.

——. *Truth Against the World.* Edited by Patrick J. Meehan. New York: John Wiley & Sons, 1987.

Wright, John Lloyd. *My Father Who is on Earth.* New York: Van Nostrand Reinhold, 1985.

PERIODICALS

Silsbee, E. A. "An Informal Talk on Architecture and Art Topics." Salem, Mass.: Essex Institute, 1880.

Wright, Frank Lloyd. "In the Cause of Architecture." *Architectural Record* 23 (March 1908): 155–221.

——. "In the Cause of Architecture." *Architectural Record* 35 (May 1914): 405–13.

1950-59

House Beautiful:
Bain House (October 1959): 244–45, 298–99.
Harmon House (November 1959): 269–70.
"Stacking Stools for Sitting and Storing" (January 1950).

1960-69

"Grotto and Geometry: House in Eden Isle, Arkansas." *Progressive Architecture* (May 1965): 142–47. (Stoneflower)

Jones, E. Fay. "Selected Details: Making Light of Wood Joinery." *Progressive Architecture* (August 1969).

"Organic Fabrication: House at Fayetteville, Arkansas." *Progressive Architecture* (May 1962): 139–42. (Jones residence)

"Palatial Rambler – Glenn Parsons House, Springdale, Arkansas." *Progressive Architecture* (May 1967): 120–23.

"Progressive Architecture's 14th Annual Design Awards Program." *Progressive Architecture* (January 1967): 158–59.

House Beautiful:
"How to Be Creative with a Saw" (January 1960).
Fletcher House (March 1960): 118–19, 161–62.
Klusmeier House (April 1962): 111–17, 186–89, 192.
Smith House (June 1962): 81–86, 159.
Snow House (October 1963): 176–80, 232–33.
Clark House (July 1964): 56–63, 108.
Pine Knoll (April 1965): 184–91, 196–98.

House Beautiful/Building Manual:
Bain House (Spring-Summer 1960).
Jones House (Spring-Summer 1961).
Smith House (Fall-Winter 1962–63).
Klusmeier House (Fall-Winter 1963–64).

House Beautiful Vacation Homes:
Fletcher House (Fall-Winter 1967).

House and Home:
Fletcher House (June 1961).
Private Residence, Bentonville, Arkansas (June 1961).
Snow House (October 1964).
Stoneflower, Arkansas (July 1966).

Life:
Stoneflower, Eden Isle, Arkansas (June 24, 1966).

Arkansas Industrial Development Commission. "This is Arkansas." March 1962. Published in *Fortune, The New Yorker, Business Weekly,* and the *Wall Street Journal.* (Clark)

1970-79

American Journal of Building Design (May 1971). (Stoneflower)

Art Voices South, January-February 1979. Article about the University of Arkansas School of Architecture. (Residences)

Edgerton, Jerry. "Making Your Dream House Come True." *Money* (September 1978): 46–47, 50–52. (Lutz)

"Homes for Better Living – Awards of Merit #18." *Housing* (August 1978). (Pallone)

Israel, Frank. "Architecture: E. Fay Jones." *Architectural Digest* (October 1978): 76–83.

"1973 Architectural Awards of Excellence of the American Institute of Steel Construction." *AIA Journal* (December 1973).

Photographic presentation of 1973 Architectural Awards of Excellence, Fourth Quarter. *Modern Steel Construction.*

"A Private Residence in Central Arkansas." *Architectural Record* (mid-May 1978): 70–71.

1980-89

Abercrombie, Stanley. "A Building of Great Integrity." *AIA Journal* (mid-May 1981): 140–47. (Thorncrown)

"Architettura: E. Fay Jones." *A.D.* (November 1982).

Cordes, Karen. "Encore Delivered with Strength & Delicacy." *Architecture* (October 1988): 52–57. (Cooper Chapel)

"A Country Home Requiring Minimal Energy Usage." *Building Stone Magazine* (July-August 1983): 20–22. (Reed)

Davis, Douglas. "A Church Is Not a Home." *Newsweek* (March 28, 1983): 76–77, 79. (Thorncrown)

Dean, A. D. "Sheltering Roof Over a Soaring Space." *Architecture* (mid-May 1984): 294–301. (Reed)

Douglas, W. L. "Poetics of Revealed Construction." *Progressive Architecture* (May 1987): 104–109. (Pinecote)

——. "E. Fay Jones: The Generative Idea." *Landscape Architecture* (May-June 1983): 68–69.

"E. Fay Jones: Roy Reed House, Hogeye, Arkansas." *Architecture & Urbanism* (July 1985): 43–46.

Fisher, T. R. "Uses of Wood Framing." *Progressive Architecture* (February 1988): 91. (Cooper Chapel)

"Frank Lloyd Wright Influenced Guest House by Fay Jones." *Architectural Lighting* (June 1989): 38.

Gandee, Charles. "Wayfarer's Chapel by Fay Jones." *Architectural Record* (March 1981): 88–93. (Thorncrown)

——. "Thorncrown Chapel, Eureka Springs, Arkansas." *Architectural Record* (March 1981): 38, 93.

Glenn, Lee. "The Personal Architecture of E. Fay Jones." *Portfolio* (Spring 1981). (Thorncrown)

Gordon, D. E. and M. S. Stubbs. "Organizing for Design Quality." *Architecture* (February 1989): 87–93.

Ivy, Robert A. "At Peace with Its Surroundings." *Architecture* (May 1988): 144–47. (Pinecote)

Jacqz, Margot. "A Sanctuary in the Woods." *Interiors* (May 1981): 176–77. (Thorncrown)

Jones, E. Fay. "Pinecote Pavilion – Crosby Arboretum, Picayune, Mississippi." *Friends of Kebyar* (April-June 1989): 8–11.

Kangas, M. "Stories from the Past." *Artweek* (March 23, 1985): 6.

Langdon, Phillip. "In the Wright Tradition." *Atlantic Monthly* (April 1989): 83–87.

Lillewitt, Susan. "Raheen: A Contemporary Castle in Arkansas." *Southern Accents* (Summer 1982): 86, 93.

"A Lyrical Environment." *Southern Accents* (March/April 1985): 108–15.

"Macchina Per Pregare." *Domus* (March 1982): 26–27.

Marlin, William. "Truing Up." *Inland Architect* (November/December 1989): 27–39.

Mays, Vernon, ed. "What Makes a Good Building." Printed lectures, College of Architecture and Urban Studies, Virginia Tech (1987): 11–12.

Moorman, M. "Artists the Critics Are Watching." *Art News* (November 1984): 95–96.

Murphy, J. "Arkansas Aerie." *Progressive Architecture* (December 1987): 88–93. (Edmondson)

"A Passive Solar Home." *Southern Accents* (Winter 1981): 56–63. (Lutz)

Plunkett, Bob. "Stonelodge, Masterpiece in Nature, Overlooks Hot Springs." *Arkansas Gazette* (March 26, 1989).

"The Projects – Fay Jones, A.I.A." *Friends of Kebyar, Inc.* (April-June 1989): 3–7. (Cooper Chapel)

Skude, Flemming. "Sadeltagets Skonhed Sapostal: om der Amerikanske Arkitect E. Fay Jones." *Arkitektur DK* (July 1987): A 150, 152, 154.

Stockman, Leslie E. "Four by Four." *Builder* (November 1986): 94–109.

"Thorncrown Chapel presso Eureka Springs, Arkansas." *L'Architettura* (December 1989): 892–93.

"Thorncrown Chapel – Architect Fay Jones." *Places* (1987): 16–17.

"Thorncrown Chapel, Bella Vista, Arkansas." *Architecture + Urbanism* (June 1981): 95–98.

"Thorncrown Chapel." *Architectural Review* (July 1981): 40–41.

"Thorncrown Chapel, Eureka Springs." *L'Architettura* (December 1981).

"Winner of the 1981 Tucker Award for Design Excellence – Robert Alexander House." *Building Stone Magazine* (May–June 1981).

"Una Gabbia (Forse) Wrightian-Chapel Eureka Springs nell Arkansas." *L'Architettura* (December 1981): 716–18.

Von Eckhardt, Wolf. "Creating for God's Glory." *Time* (April 1982).

White, Mel. "The Master Builder." *Arkansas Times* (November 1983).

"Winner of the 1982 Tucker Architectural Award for Design Excellence – Thorncrown Chapel." *Building Stone Magazine* (March/April 1982).

"Wrightiana al Tatio." *L'Architettura* (November 1984): 812–13.

1990-92

"A.I.A. Gold Medal Winners." *Architectural Record* (February 1990): 5.

Branch, M. A. "Fay Jones Wins A.I.A. Gold Medal." *Progressive Architecture* (January 1990): 27.

Dillon, David. "Grandeur in a Small Place." *Dallas Morning News* (December 5, 1990). (Leonard Chapel)

"E. Fay Jones, A.I.A. Gold Medalist." *Architectural Record* (April 1990): 15.

"Following Wright Principles." *Kitchen & Bath Concepts* (January 1990): 34–39. (Grober)

Ivy, Robert A. "Solid Gold (American Institute of Architecture's Gold Medalist)." *Architecture* (March 1990): 82–89.

Jones, E. Fay. "The 1990 Gold Medal Address." *Architectural Record* (April 1990): 21. (Watson, Thorncrown Worship Center)

"Major Review of Fayetteville, Arkansas, Architect – Winner of the A.I.A's Medal (Watson, Pinecote, Thorncrown)." *Architecture* (March 1990): 82–89.

Nesmith, L. "E. Fay Jones Presented Institute's Highest Honor." *Architecture* (January 1990): 25.

"News: Fay Jones is First Taliesin Fellow to Receive A.I.A.Gold Medal." *Journal of Taliesin Fellows* (Spring 1990): 4–5.

"Operative Opposites – Using Steel within the Traditional Geometry of Gothic Design Created a Dramatically Airy Structure." *Modern Steel Construction* (March/April 1990): 22–26. (Cooper Chapel)

"Watson Residence: Organic Testimony." *L'Architettura* (September 1990): 642–43.

ACKNOWLEDGMENTS

Writing Fay Jones's book has been happy labor, since Fay and Gus Jones made each trip to Arkansas a homecoming for me. I regret, in some sense, completing this effort, since my excuses for traveling to Fayetteville will decrease.

To Fay Jones's partner, Maurice Jennings, to Dave McKee, and to the rest of Jones's staff, I owe a special debt. Invariably willing when called upon, they sought out forgotten drawings, answered telephone queries, and sat with me past office hours into the dark.

Joel Stein, former editor of the AIA Press, invited me to write this book, and I owe him a hearty thank you. His publisher, John Hoke, cemented the bond with encouragement, a contract, and bountiful conversation. He handed me over to managing editor Cynthia Ware who offered cheerfulness and helpful advice through two years of work. She obtained Allen Freeman's help in editing the text, and he improved it in every case. Janet Rumbarger oversaw its production and suffered through messy emendations with good humor and precision. Pamela James Blumgart ensured the accuracy of final editing.

Mississippian Joan Embree acted as researcher, bibliographer, and amanuensis. Careful readers like architectural historian Patrick Snadon tied down loosely floating facts. Erika Morrison assisted with research chores. Libraries at Mississippi State University and the University of Arkansas lent substantial aid. My former assistant, Laura Holmes, now living in Little Rock, helped bring order to a chaotic world. Randy Anderson and Rick Mordecai loyally maintained my architectural practice, freeing many mornings for writing.

The book's designers, Brad Collins, Diane Kasprowicz, and Cheryl Towler, carried a sympathetic understanding of the subject through the book's framework, thereby allowing Jones's work to shine through. Groups of people helped. All of the photographers whose work fills this book dug into their archives for Fay Jones's work. His loyal clients opened their homes for me on wet weekend days and fielded numerous telphone interviews.

My family was bedrock support. My mother, Frances Ivy, read the manuscript and knew how to spell "amanuensis." My father, Robert Ivy, offered unqualified help, as did my children—Virginia, Adam, and Ben—who respected my need for a quiet room. No one supported me in this effort more than my wife, Holly. She made a tangible sacrifice as she encouraged me to stay home mornings to write while she went off to work.

Everyone who knows Fay Jones, and a few who did not, wanted to help. Thanks to you all.

PHOTO CREDITS

All photographs and drawings are provided courtesy of Fay Jones and Maurice Jennings, Architects. Individual photographers are credited at right.

Photograph of *Above the Clouds at Sunrise,* p. 23, provided courtesy of the Warner Collection of the Gulf States Paper Corporation, Tuscaloosa, Alabama.

PAUL BESWICK / BESWICK INTERNATIONAL

Raheen: all; *Lutz:* all (except p. 156)

EDWARD L. BLAKE JR.

Pinecote Pavilion: p. 76, 81, 86 (upper left), 87, 88 (upper right)

MICHAEL BRUCE / MAGUIRE-REEDER, LTD.

The Evolution of Principles: p. 17, 20; *Edmondson Residence:* p. 164 (lower left)

RODNEY DUNGAN

Private Residence, northwest Arkansas: p. 137 (top); *Private Residence outside Little Rock, Arkansas:* all (except p. 149, 153)

LYNN GAMMILL

Pinecote Pavilion: p. 80

GREG HURSLEY

Jones's Place in Contemporary Architecture: p. 13; *Thorncrown Chapel:* p. 40, 42–45 (except upper right, p. 42); *Marty Leonard Chapel:* all; *Edmondson Residence:* all (except lower left, p. 164); *Reed Residence:* all

TIMOTHY HURSLEY

Introduction: p. 11; *The Evolution of Principles:* p. 26; *Thorncrown Chapel:* p. 32–34, 37; *Thorncrown Worship Center:* all, except p. 50; *Cooper Chapel:* p. 52, 53, 55–59, 61, 65, 66; *Pinecote Pavilion:* p. 77–79, 82–86 (except upper left, p. 86), 88–91 (except upper right, p. 88); *Pine Eagle:* all; *Stoneflower:* p. 118; *Private Residence, northwest Arkansas:* 128–135, 137 (lower right); *Davenport Residence:* all; *Watson Residence:* all

BALTHAZAR KORAB

Jones Residence: p. 102–103 (lower right); *Stoneflower:* all (except p. 118); *Monaghan Residence:* all; *Design of Houses:* p. 200–201, 204–205

MARVIN RAND

The Evolution of Principles: p. 28

ROSENTHAL ART SLIDES

The Evolution of Principles: p. 16, 18, 19, 29

WAYNE SORCE

Thorncrown Chapel: p. 35, 36, 38–39, 41, 42 (upper right); *Thorncrown Worship Center:* p. 50; *Cooper Chapel:* p. 54, 62, 63

EZRA STOLLER / ESTO

Pine Knoll: all; *Design of Houses:* p. 206, 208–209